Saddle Your Own Horse

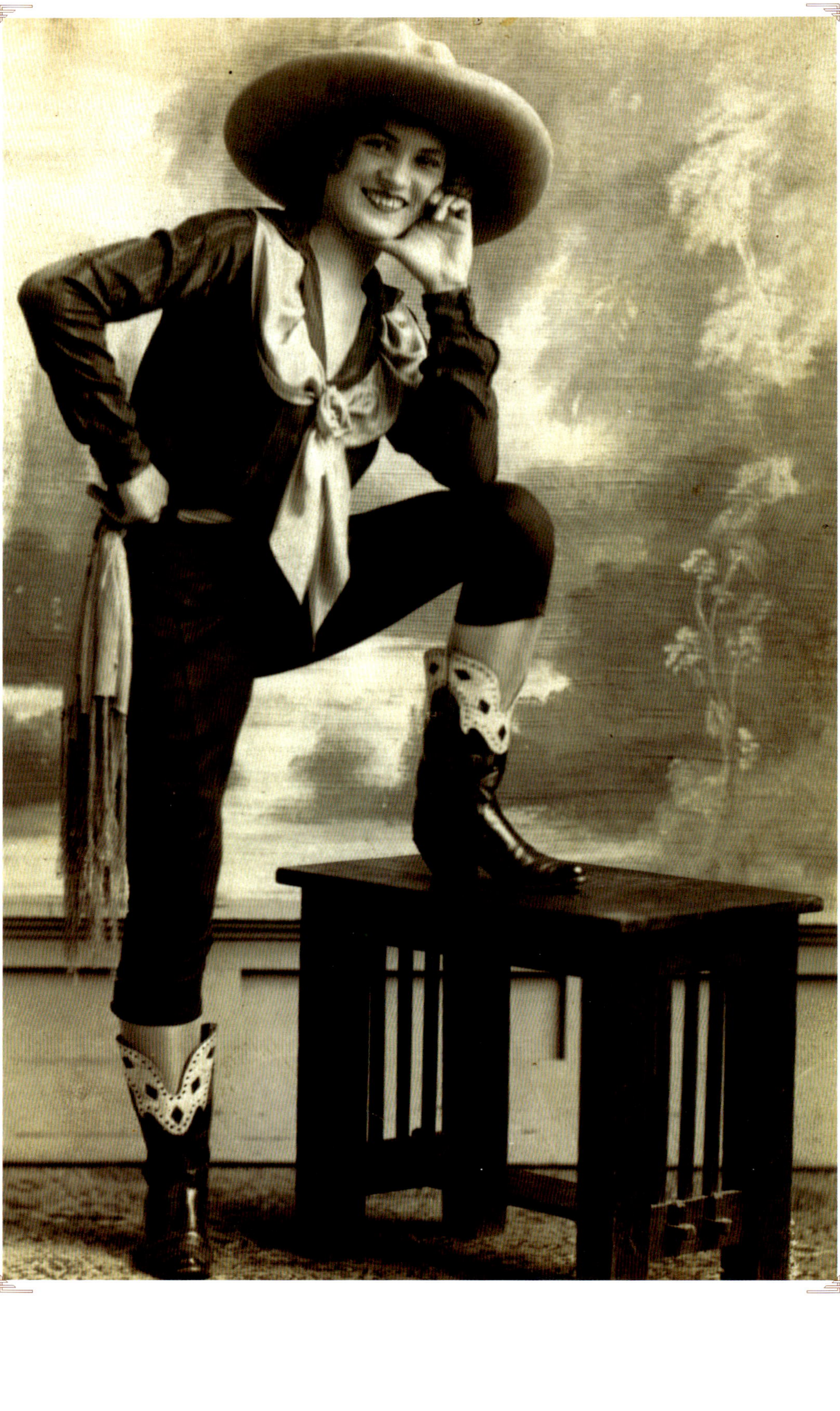

Saddle Your Own Horse

A Tribute to Cowgirls and the Cowgirl Spirit

NATIONAL COWGIRL MUSEUM AND HALL OF FAME

*The National Cowgirl Museum
and Hall of Fame honors and
documents the lives of women who
have distinguished themselves
while exemplifying the
pioneer spirit of
the American West.*

Copyright 2002 by the National Cowgirl Museum and Hall of Fame
All rights reserved. Reproduction in any form is prohibited without specific permission.

ISBN 0-9719508-0-6

Table of Contents

Introduction	9
Artifacts and Collections	11
The National Cowgirl Museum and Hall of Fame	16
Into the Arena	22
Kinship with the Land	32
Claiming the Spotlight	40
Acknowledgements	48
Credits	49
Honorees	54
Messages from our Supporters	69

Cowgirl is an attitude, really.

A pioneer spirit,

A special American brand of courage.

The cowgirl faces life head on,

lives by her own lights,

and makes no excuses.

Cowgirls take stands, they speak up.

They defend things they hold dear.

Dale Evans

Introduction

Angels in the Saddle

*Like the women it honors,
this new museum defies expectations*

Pendleton, 1923. Anticipation rippled through the crowd like a breeze as a lone figure entered the arena on horseback. Head down, the rider picked up speed. The powerful chestnut stallion went to full gallop, and as horse and rider passed in front of the viewing stand, the rider suddenly leaped off the horse into the air, landing back in the saddle on one foot, the other somehow looped into the reins.

The crowd erupted in an amazed roar as the rider now leaned back, arms outstretched, like a dancer in full repose. But the best surprise was yet to come. Out from under the enormous cowboy hat came not the gritty visage of a hardened cowboy, mustached and weather-beaten, but the face of an angel. Here, at the muddy brown center of an Oregon rodeo, flashed a magnificent smile framed by shimmering red lipstick.

Her name was Mabel Strickland, and into the untamed wild of the early American West, she and her contemporaries brought color, romance and courage. Some, like Mabel, rode saddle broncs and roped steers; others wrote books, built businesses or, like Georgia O'Keeffe, worked magic with a paintbrush. Collectively, we call them cowgirls, women of character and grit who, outnumbered in those early days almost seven-to-one by their male counterparts, managed to make this new frontier not just a place to survive, but to thrive.

Almost a century later, the cowgirl is alive and kicking, pluckier than ever. Today she might wield a cell phone and drive a sport utility vehicle, but she carries in her heart that same spirit of adventure. Like her sisters before her, she rides into each day with a passion for life and an underlying strength that comes from healthy self-reliance. As Connie Reeves put it, a cowgirl "always saddles her own horse".

I was present when a handful of those modern day cowgirls set out to raise $21 million to build this museum. Led by a devoted team and a dynamic board, they got the job done over the next four years. But even more impressive is what they created: a radiant, soaring tribute of a museum that goes far beyond what you will expect. While classic and grand, it is not so much a building as it is a living space, full of vital, encouraging tributes to unforgettable people. It also has a delightful sense of humor. Most of all, it is relevant. Relevant to all of us—women and men—struggling to make our way in this newer, more complex frontier.

One visit and you'll know that the National Cowgirl Museum and Hall of Fame is a truly unique place, dedicated to a very special class of wondrous women. Until then, don't underestimate the cowgirl; under her hat, she holds many surprises

Reid Slaughter
Publisher & Executive Editor
Cowboys & Indians Magazine

Clockwise from top left: chaps and vest worn by rancher Ruby Gobble as a child; chaps worn by champion cowgirl Gene Creed, circa 1930's; split skirt worn by Gertrude Maxwell, circa 1900-1910; custom-tailored Nudie shirt, skirt, and vest worn by Dale Evans.

Facing page: Wild West outfit, circa 1890

Artifacts and Collections

Saddles! Spurs! Trophies! Ribbons! Photographs! Letters! Posters!

These constitute the permanent collection of the National Cowgirl Museum and Hall of Fame. It is an irreplaceable legacy. Each artifact, each piece of memorabilia tells its own story, but together they speak volumes about the cowgirl spirit and the women who are honored here.

When these treasures come together in our galleries, they create lasting connections with our visitors by communicating the richness and complexity of cowgirl life. Indeed, it is both glamorous and grand and as heartbreaking as it is rewarding. For example, in the permanent collection is the cast that trick rider Ruth Roach wore after breaking her leg in 1933. The cast tells visitors of the dangers and risks of rodeo, but the inscriptions on it – the clever poems and cheery comments – by her fellow cowgirls reveal the depth of love and fellowship of rodeo competitors. The red boots Jan Youren wore while winning the Bareback Bronc Riding World Championship in 1987 also tell a story. Now tattered and torn, they reflect the hard work each successful rodeo rider must experience and endure.

The importance of this collection is its range and breadth. Here, a visitor will find everything from a hoof pick, to a rhinestone saddle, to a black-ware pot by Maria Martinez. Although such items are not often found under the same roof, here they help tell the stories of the women who have lived the cowgirl life, the women who have made the cowgirl an unforgettable American icon, and the women who personify the cowgirl spirit.

Started in Hereford in 1975, the collection now exceeds 2,000 artifacts, 3,000 photographs, 1,500 books, and reams of archival documents. It has grown through the generosity and help of many honorees and their families, who have shared their lives and donated their belongings, and it has benefited from the expertise and advice given by collectors as well as the vision and talents given by the founders and donors to the Museum. Their efforts have combined to make the permanent collection an integral part of this wonderful institution where incredible stories and lives are brought together, cared for and shared with the world.

Gold leather and rhinestone saddle designed by Nudie for Judy Lynn

Nudie designed two saddles for me. The first was black with, like, half a million rhinestones; then he did a gold leather one with half a million rhinestones. The only time I got a lump in my throat was when I got out of show business and I sold that saddle.

Judy Lynn

Augusta Metcalfe's leather sidesaddle made in 1899

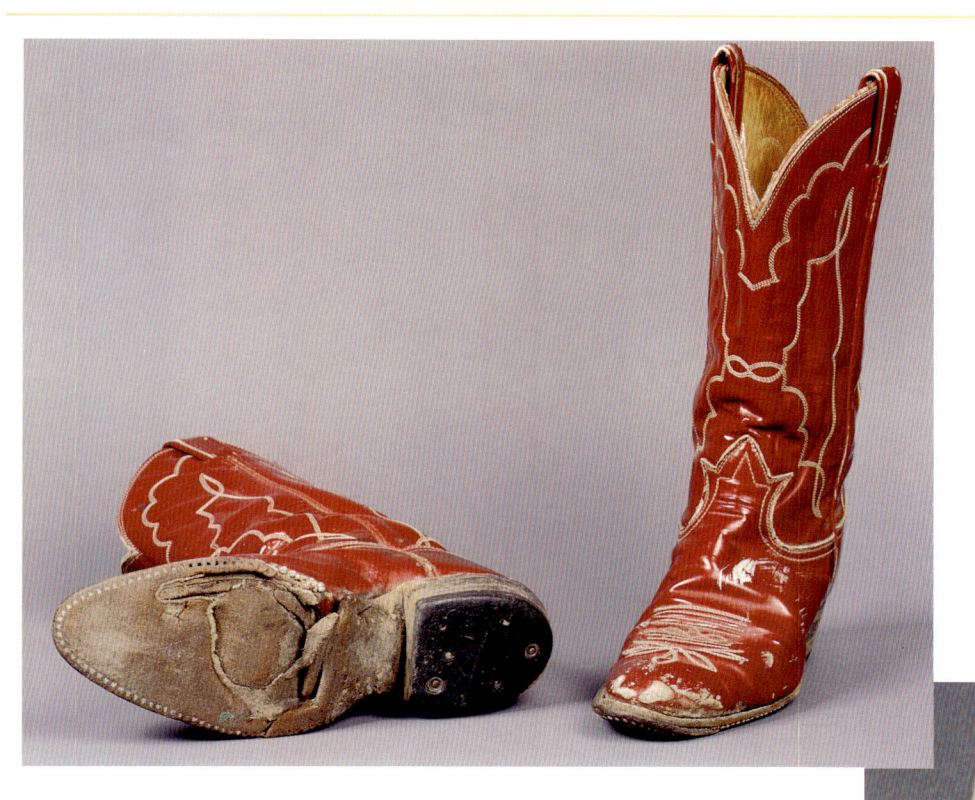

All my new boots start out as my dancing boots until they get holes in the soles, then I drop them in my rigging bag and they become my riding boots, and I ride 'em until they fall clear apart.

Jan Youren

The cast at right, worn by champion cowgirl Ruth Roach in 1933, bears numerous inscriptions including the following two:

Never say stop in a mudhole.

*This cast contains one leg
The leg does not belong in the cast
To truly appreciate this leg
You should see it in a saddle
as I saw it.*

Bootmaking is an art, and we continue doing a lot of the work by hand. Our people take the same pride in workmanship that made my father's boots so popular before the turn of the century.

Enid Justin

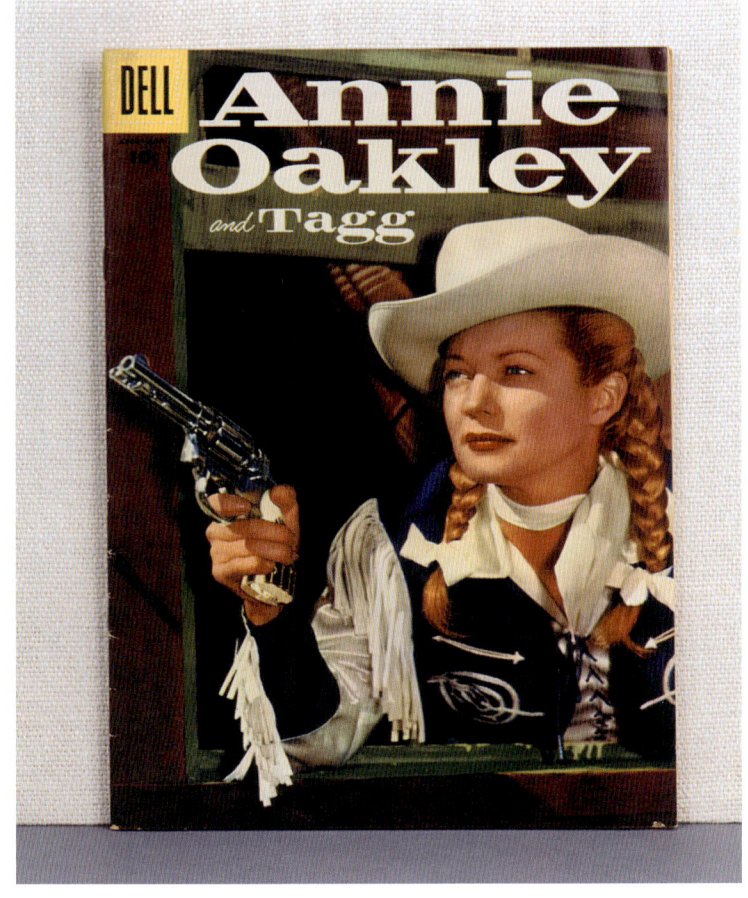

Counterclockwise from top:

1956 comic book from the popular television show "Annie Oakley"; this upright bass, made for Laura Lynch Tull by Robert Lee of Cleveinger, takes the form of a sagurao cactus; cowgirls were popular figures on tobacco tins

Right: detail from a vintage Nudie shirt worn by Laura Lynch Tull

Above right: a spectacular hat thought to be designed by Nudie

Below: a pair of spurs any cowgirl would be proud to wear

Left: a bronc riding trophy won by Gene Creed at the 1934 Southwestern Exposition and Fat Stock Show

The National Cowgirl Museum and Hall of Fame

As much as any other era in American History, the days of the Wild West capture the public's imagination with an enduring sense of adventure and discovery. Whether recalled through fiction or through fact, this period was awe-inspiring in its instances of triumph over daunting forces of nature and undeniably romantic in its tales of exceptional courage, cunning and iron-willed determination to tame the wilderness.

The names of men who personify the western frontier are universally recognized: Wild Bill Hickok, Geronimo, Kit Carson, Buffalo Bill Cody, Sitting Bull and a host of others. History has been much less generous, however, in recording the exploits and contributions of frontier women. Annie Oakley, Calamity Jane, Sacajawea, Belle Starr and a few others are familiar names that, like their male counterparts, have become icons of American history. Still other women - including Willa Cather, Laura Ingalls Wilder and Georgia O'Keeffe have created enduring works of art and literature that depict and chronicle this fascinating era.

More recently, show business has portrayed such immortals as Patsy Cline and Dale Evans. But there are countless unsung women who were part and parcel of the western experience: rodeo cowgirls, homemakers and ranch hands who lived by their wits and toiled from dawn to dusk in the service of community, home and family.

In 1975, realizing that women of the American West and their accomplishments had been largely overlooked, a visionary group led by Margaret C. Formby established a museum, the National Cowgirl Hall of Fame and Western Heritage Center, in the basement of the Deaf Smith County Library in the Texas Panhandle community of Hereford. Its purpose was to honor and document the lives of legendary women who have distinguished themselves while exemplifying the pioneer spirit of the American West.

Almost 20 years later, because of increasing interest in the museum and the fact that the available audience for this important program was limited in the Hereford location, the board initiated a search for alternative sites that promised greater audience exposure and more opportunity for an expanded and improved public education program. When Fort Worth community and business leaders learned of the possibility of moving the museum to Fort Worth, they sought to make it a reality, and in 1994 the move was made and plans were under way to build a new permanent home.

On February 22, 2001, hundreds of spectators and more than 160 women on horseback gathered to break ground for the new 33,000-square-foot museum. Eighteen months later, Grand Opening festivities for the Cowgirl's new home were held between June 6-9, 2002. At that time, 158 women had been inducted into the Cowgirl Hall of Fame, of whom many were present to witness the extraordinary debut of the institution built to honor them and the value system they embodied.

Almost six years before the National Cowgirl Museum and Hall of Fame opened to the public, its world-class design and construction team was already in place. David M. Schwarz/Architectural Services, Inc., design architect, and Linbeck Construction Company, with Tom Hale as project director and Brian Broom as project manager, would build the building. Vicki Dickerson, president of Sundance Projects Group, would provide project management, ensuring the museum's completion on time, on budget and with the highest quality. The companies had previously worked together for more than 10 years and had achieved extraordinary success creating several beautiful, state-of-the-art buildings in Fort Worth, including the Nancy Lee and Perry R. Bass Performance Hall. For its part, David M. Schwarz/Architectural Services, Inc. had a threefold goal in its design: to relate the building to the historic context of the site, to create a vibrant new space as the home for the National Cowgirl Museum and Hall of Fame and to provide expansion possibilities for the museum as its collections grow. The building's location near the historic Will Rogers Center in the Fort Worth Cultural District and its conception as a key part of the Western Heritage Center (to be formed by the Cowgirl Museum, the Cattle Raisers Museum and the Fort Worth Museum of Science and History), helped determine the style, materials and architectural forms of the building.

The style of the building is compatible with the Modern style of the Will Rogers Center. The exterior is brick and cast stone with terra cotta finials formed in a wild-rose motif and glazed in vibrant colors. A large painted mural by Richard Haas and bas-relief sculpture panels by Montage show scenes related to the Cowgirl's story, depict thematic messages such as East Meets West and Saddle Your Own Horse and represent the story told inside the museum.

The museum's interior houses administrative offices, three gallery areas, a multipurpose theater, hands-on children's areas, a flexible exhibit space, a research library, a catering area and the gift store. The store, designed by Pat Enstrom, is dedicated to Cowgirl honoree Mamie Francis Hafley and her Wild West Show diving horse act. A 45-foot-high domed rotunda serves as a constant orienting point and houses the Hall of Fame honoree exhibits. Two grand staircases providing exceptional overlooks into the rotunda at the ground floor are made of different metal finishes and colors with Art Deco inspired ornamental railings. Twelve LIFETILE murals, animated ribbed glass tiles created by artist Rufus Seder, ring the perimeter of the rotunda at ground level.

The exhibit spaces, designed by West Office Exhibit Design, are created to present the museum as a three-dimensional scrapbook full of remarkable stories of remarkable women, with the overarching theme of the spirit of the cowgirl. The second floor rotunda, a beautifully designed space, reveals the many attributes of the cowgirl through words, images and artifacts and introduces the concept of the spirit-trail lariat that continues throughout the museum. The *Claiming the Spotlight* gallery focuses on cowgirls in popular culture, enveloping visitors in a fast paced and dynamic world of images from film, television, advertising, literature and music. In the *Kinship with the Land* gallery, visitors survey the vast expanses of the horizon as they experience both the harshness and the beauty of the land and hear first-hand accounts of the trials and tribulations of the women who made their lives there. *Into the Arena* tells the story of the great cowgirl champions and fills visitors with adrenaline as they witness the greatest rides in history on three swinging projection screens that rotate much like the gate of a rodeo chute.

A wonderful new home has been created for the National Cowgirl Museum and Hall of Fame and the future is bright.

What has been built in Fort Worth, Texas, is more than walls and a roof – it is a home for the stories of the remarkable women who have contributed so significantly to American history. It is a place where these stories can be housed, preserved and made available to the thousands of people from around the world who will visit the museum each year.

One of the brightest aspects of the National Cowgirl Museum and Hall of Fame's future is the unlimited educational opportunities that lie ahead. Children of all ages will be able to experience and learn about the amazing history and lives of the women featured in the museum in a setting that is sure to educate, engage and entertain. For children who can't visit the facility, the museum's outreach education program will take the museum experience to them! Schools and groups across the country will be able to access the various outreach programs, from traveling education trunks to programs designed to allow children to research and nominate candidates to the Hall of Fame.

The museum's future strength and growth are also involved with its ever growing and expanding research facility. Recently, an oral history program has been established allowing the Museum to document the histories of the living honorees as well as other significant western women. These stories are being recorded and preserved in formats that include video, audio and written transcriptions. The stories being preserved by this program are vital to the preservation of this history.

And just as this history is still developing, so is the museum. As women continue to blaze trails and determine the course of Western life, the museum will continue to document their stories and contributions. For, just as America and the West continue to change and develop, so does the cowgirl. Today she lives in the city as well as the country. She pilots a plane as well as rides a horse. She runs a bank as well as manages a ranch. She has that cowgirl spirit inherited from the generations of remarkable women who went before her, and she is using it to pioneer new worlds from the Supreme Court to new technologies. Some things never change. She still always saddles her own horse...has and always will.

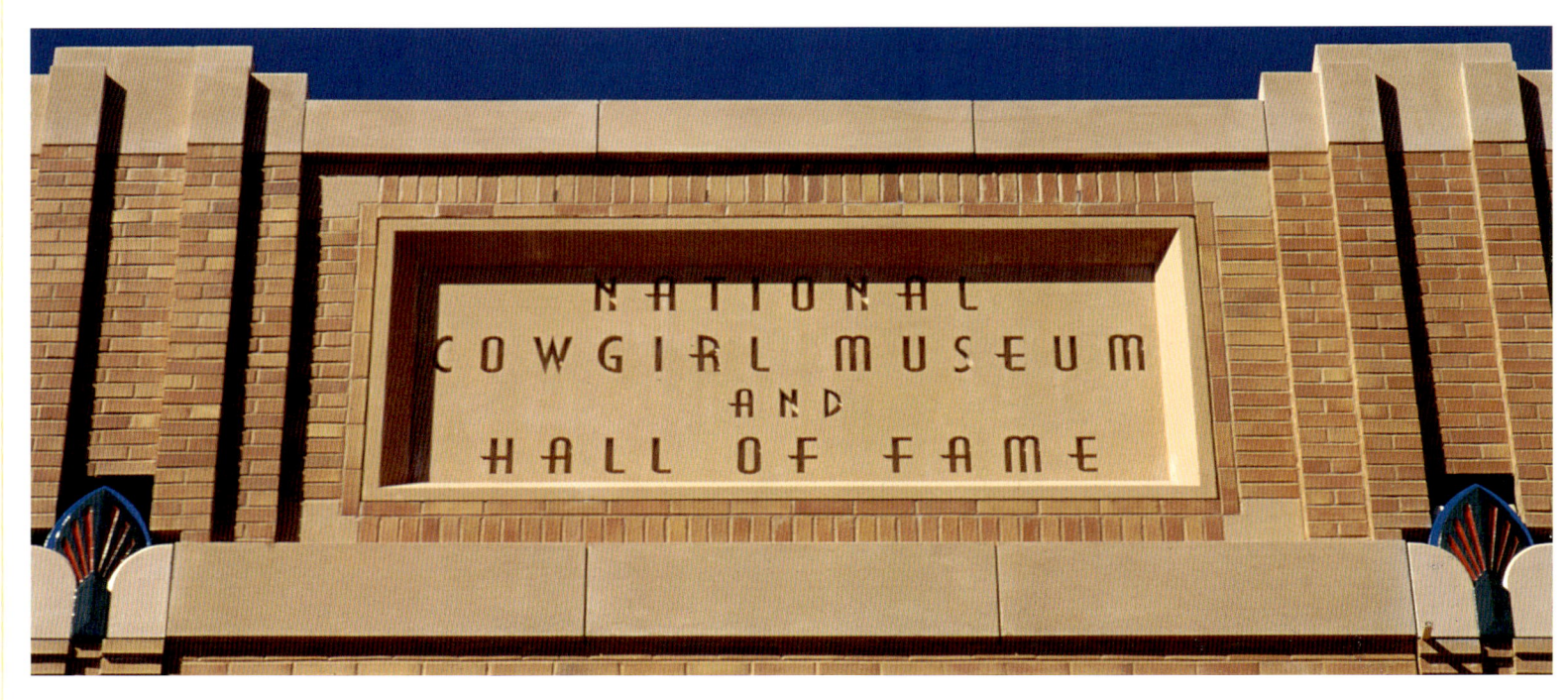

The Spirit of the Cowgirl Galleries

The *Into The Arena* Gallery

Fancy Riding by Tillie Baldwin Champion Lady Buckaroo

*I'm happiest when my hair is blowing behind me
and I'm galloping at a breakneck speed in the arena.*

Mildred Mulhall

Anyone who likes roulette ought to like cutting.

Helen Groves

Barrel Racing

It's not about money. Or having nice things. It's about knowing yourself and that the hard work you did paid off.

Charmayne James

Speed

You've got to concentrate on that will to win as much as anything. I think the will to win is most important. If you're mounted, you've got to sit back there and say, "I can win if I want to, if I give it my best shot." You've got to concentrate like that run after run after run.

Lynn McKenzie

But, I found out that you didn't get the "how to" until you got the "want to." I definitely had the "want to" to be a barrel racer.

Martha Josey

Golden Age

I maintain that every act of daring performed in public contributes something to the sum of human courage.

Mamie Francis Hafley

*We came from a great era.
We call ourselves the Wild Bunch.*

Alice Greenough

MARJORIE BOYSEN-TRICK AND FANCY

We all had a lot of clothes. We always wore our best clothes, no matter what we were doing. If we had to ride a bull, or a bucking horse, or anything else, we wore our best clothes, we sure did.

Tad Lucas

The biggest thrill I ever had in my life was the ride up out of that basement [Madison Square Garden] in this monstrous great big building filled with thousands of people. If that wasn't something for a little ole country gal to see for the first time!

Alice Greenough

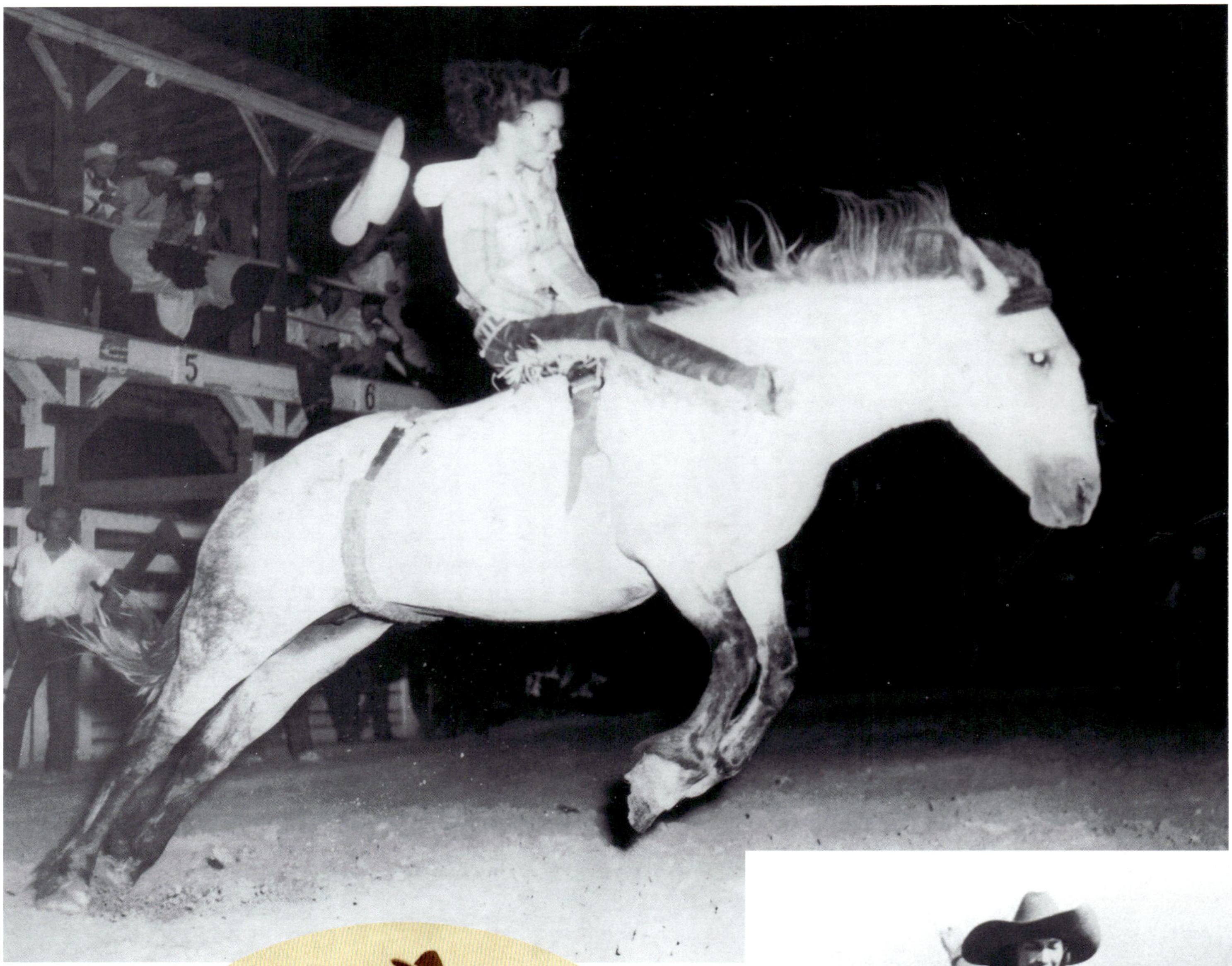

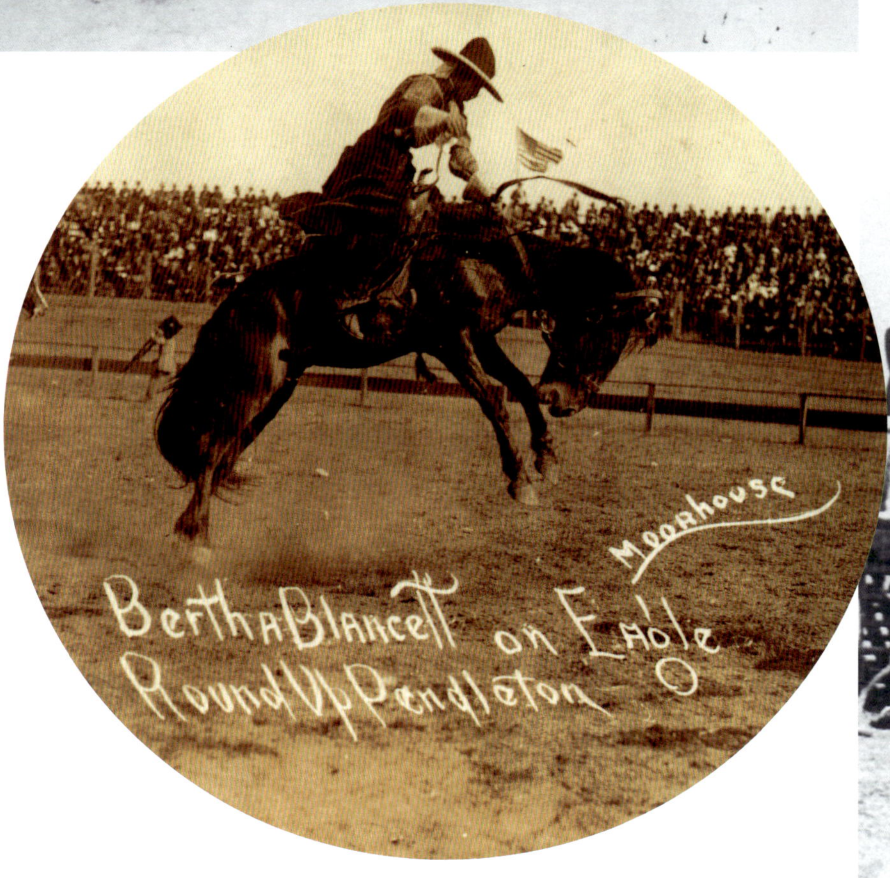
Moorhouse
Bertha Blancett on Eagle
Round Up Pendleton O

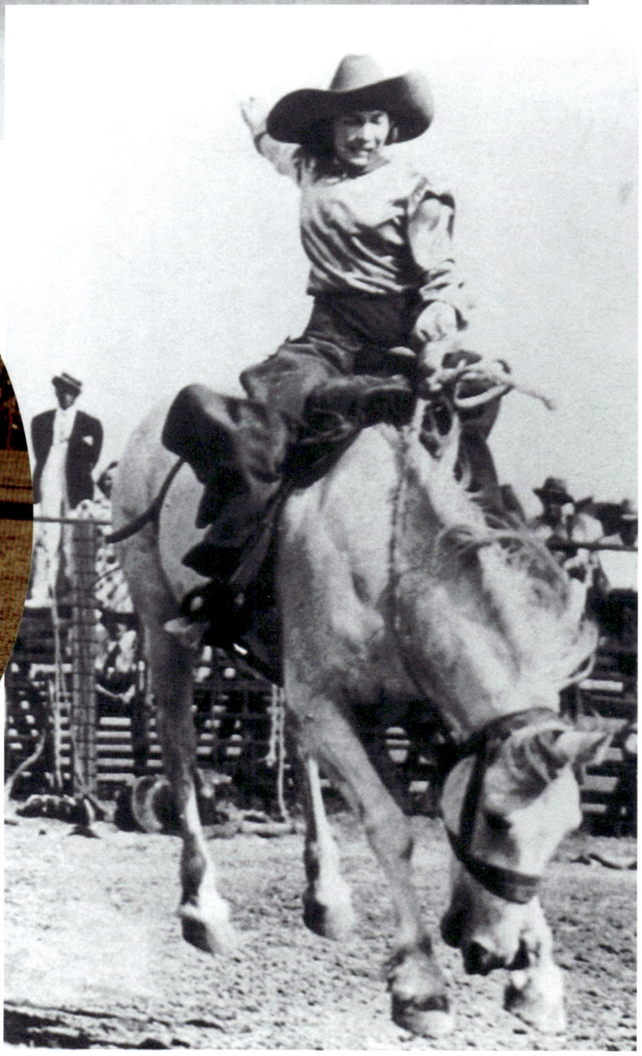

When I was a girl, it wasn't a girl's place to be riding a bucking horse. Out there in the arena, they thought it was the wrong thing to be a doin'. I was one of those people that didn't care what people thought. I did it anyway.

Bobby Brooks Kramer

I don't remember whether it was a full buck or just part of a buck. Anyway, I started on my first aerial journey and received my first lesson in astronomy. Did I see stars? Well, I'm personally acquainted with each and every one of them, from Jupiter to Mars.

Bertha Blancett

Daring

Wild West Shows

Let any normally healthy woman who is ordinarily strong screw up her courage and tackle a bucking bronco, and she will find the most fascinating pastime in the field of feminine athletic endeavor. There is nothing to compare, to increase the joy of living, and once accomplished, she'll have more real fun than any pink tea or theater party ever yielded.

May Lillie, star of Pawnee Bill's Wild West Show

There was something left of the Wild West in rodeo. Riding a good bronc makes you feel like hollering "Ye Haw!"

Jan Youren

Boots

All I need is cattle, a good horse, a pick-up truck and a good pair of boots.

Fern Sawyer

I warn people when I give them a pair of boots, that they'll grow on you... that they're habit-forming. I tell them that if they don't want to become addicted, they'd better not wear them.

John Justin

The Kinship with the Land Gallery

*The land is our trial, our comfort,
and ultimately our identity.*

Robyn Carmichael Eden

This is a story told by the Cooksley sisters:

There were so many more men than women in those days that proposals were a common thing.

One day a cowboy rode up to the house, came inside and asked, "will you marry me?" The sisters responded, "which one of us are you asking?" His reply was, "either one of you."

34

I grew up on a small ranch in a nowhere place called Hasty, Colorado. I loved it. My horse, Risky, and I would go riding near every day. I took long walks over to my cousins' house where them and I would stack hay 'til late at night, or 'til it was too dark to see. Then we'd get on top of the stack and listen to the coyotes howling. Then we'd all jump in the pickup and go spotlighting. Even when my brother and I were riding fence, I loved it. In the middle of snowstorms I'd go out and stay with the horses, since the electricity was out anyway. I even got bowed legs already. If things were different, I'd be back in Colorado right now, probably splitting wood or riding Risky through three-foot-deep snow, unless she had bucked me off. I was only half-done breaking her when I had to leave. One day soon, I'm going back for good.

Tammy Jo Smigh

Split Skirt

Although my costume was so full as to look like an ordinary walking dress when the wearer was on foot, it created a small sensation. So great at first was the prejudice against any divided garment in Montana that a warning was given me to abstain from riding in the streets of Miles City lest I might be arrested! After riding into town forty-eight miles from the ranch, I was much amused at the laughing and giggling first who stood staring at my costume as I walked about.

Evelyn Cameron

Comfort and protection soon became more important in my dress than looks or what others thought.

Hallie Crawford Stillwell

Side Saddle

My own great concession to the new age was to abandon the sidesaddle. Why for ten years, I continued to ride sidesaddle is a mystery to me now.

Agnes Morley Cleaveland

Film

I curled up in the bedroll and thought about the peaceful night, warm with a light stir of a cool breeze. I heard the squeak of the wooden wheel on the windmill as it turned. Once in a while, I heard a coyote yip in the distance or a mother cow bawling for her calf. The hypnotic rhythm of the windmill should have put me to sleep, but it didn't. The remarks I had overheard that evening were still too fresh on my mind. My hipbones ached as I turned from side to side attempting to get comfortable. My mind remained active. I wondered what my role as a pioneer ranch wife would be like. This man lying next to me had had such a different life from mine.

Hallie Crawford Stillwell

Saddle Your Own Horse

The whole part of being a cowgirl is being able to handle hard work. A cowgirl is growing up with that kind of life and knowing how it feels to fall off an animal and get right back up. When you really love horses, the work doesn't seem like that much, but it really is.

Cam Phillips

We were not over-indulged with toys and play gadgets. We used our imaginations and improvised.

Stephanie Prepiora

Independent

The *Claiming the Spotlight* Gallery

Dale Evans made a cowgirl out of me.

The Dixie Chicks, "Thank Heavens for Dale Evans"

Advertising

The cowgirl signified the freedom to move about life above ground level, to "get away from it all," to make her own decisions about where she wanted to go and how she wanted to get there and to fill more than one role with optimism, enthusiasm, skill and intense love of life.

Joyce Gibson Roach

Dressing The Stars

Nudie knew exactly what was needed for show. His outfits weighed a ton because of all the rhinestones but boy did they glitter in the lights.

Gail Davis

Dazzling

43

Television

Little boys have their idols. Why not give the girls a western star of their own?

Gene Autry

Music

I've always liked songs about strong women.   Reba McEntire

Movies

**SHE STRIPS OFF HER PETTICOATS
...and straps on her guns!**

BARBARA STANWYCK
woman of fire...in a land aflame!

RONALD REAGAN
dangerous friend...deadly foe!

CATTLE QUEEN
OF MONTANA

PRINT BY **TECHNICOLOR**

Pop Fiction

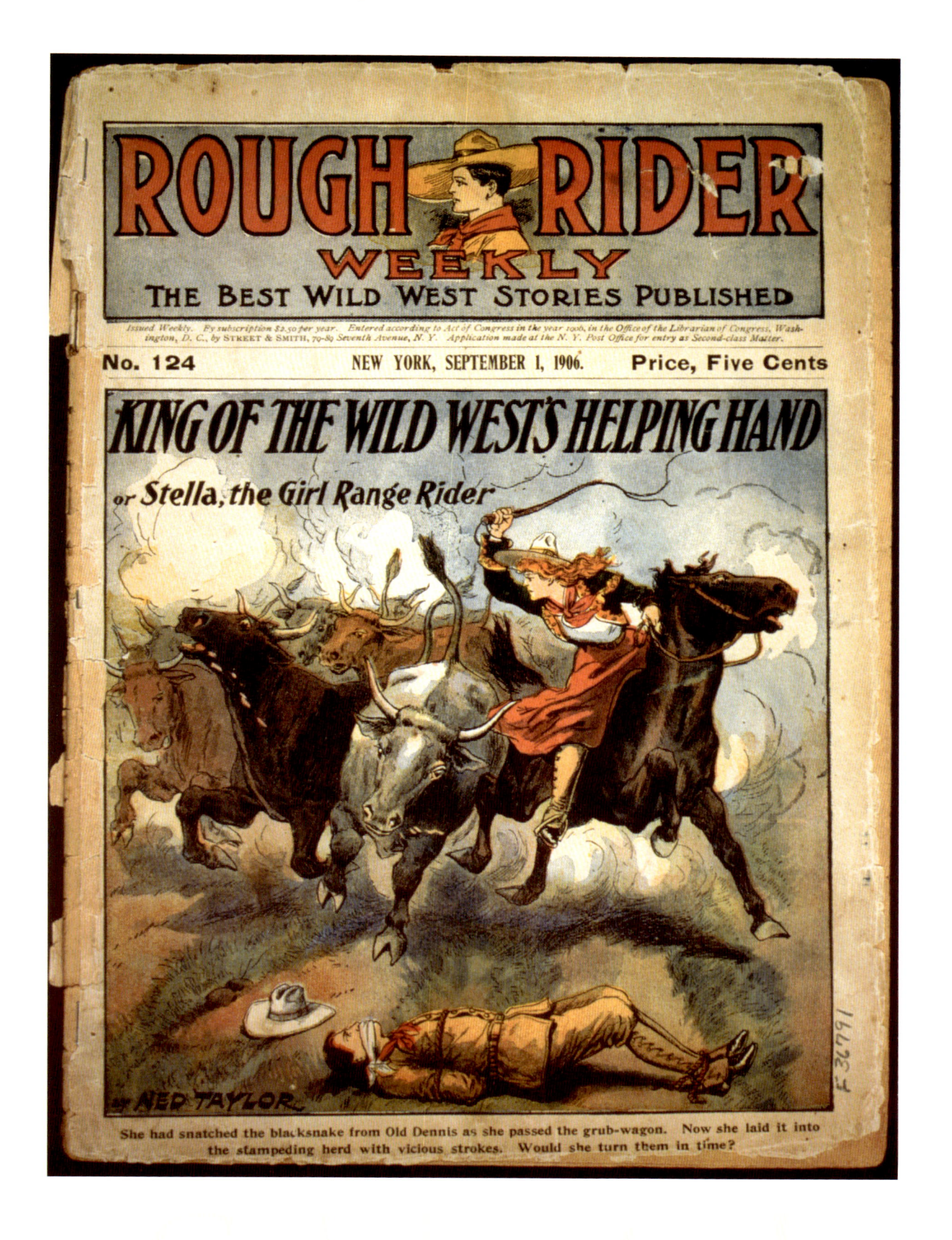

ROUGH RIDER WEEKLY
THE BEST WILD WEST STORIES PUBLISHED

No. 124   NEW YORK, SEPTEMBER 1, 1906.   Price, Five Cents

KING OF THE WILD WEST'S HELPING HAND
or Stella, the Girl Range Rider

She had snatched the blacksnake from Old Dennis as she passed the grub-wagon. Now she laid it into the stampeding herd with vicious strokes. Would she turn them in time?

Acknowledgements

BOARD OF DIRECTORS

Kit T. Moncrief – President
Vicki S. Bass – Vice President
William V. Boecker – Vice President
Windi Grimes – Vice President
Carol J. Beech – Secretary
Denise A. Spitler – Treasurer
Elaine B. Agather – Member at Large
Joline M. Wharton – Member at Large

H. B. (Hub) Baker
Jil T. Barnes
Janie Beggs
Judy Beggs Clement
Kevin S. Downing
Georgia Mae Ericson
Gilbert Gamez, Jr.
Paula Gaughan
Kay Gay
Toni Geren
Jimmie Gibbs-Munroe
Sue Hearst
Kate Johnson
Mary Lester
Nancy B. Loeffler
Roberta Louckx
Mary Ralph Lowe
Teddi Marks
Stacie McDavid
Robin S. Merrill
Lesa Oudt
Mary Martha Richter
Mitzi Riley
Bridget Trenary
Laura Tull
Wanda Waters
Jerri M. Watt
Martha Williams

ADVISORY BOARD

Tobin Armstrong
William Arrington
Edward P. Bass
Anne Brockington
First Lady Laura Bush
The Honorable Susan Combs
Richard L. Connor
Dan J. Craine
Alvin G. Davis
Sherry Delamarter
Cass O. Edwards, II
Caroline A. Forgason
Debbie Garrison
Walt Garrison
The Honorable Kay Granger
Linda Gray
Helen K. Groves
Doug Harman
George C. Hixon
The Honorable Kay Bailey Hutchison
Roxanne Johnson
Nathalie Kent
Edith McAllister
Reba N. McEntire
Larry Mahan
Anne W. Marion
Maggie Messman
Pam Minick
Steve Murrin, Jr.
Kathleen Newton
Wayne Newton
Anita Perry
Hilton Queton
Van Romans
Carol Rose
Mrs. Randolph Scott
Jerry Portwood Taylor
W. R. Watt, Jr.
Buster Welch

Lifetime Honorary Member -
Margaret Formby

STAFF

Patricia W. Riley, Executive Director
Jennifer E. Nielsen, Curator
Susan Fine, Director of Development and Marketing
Mary Etta Cochran, Director of Finance
Emmy Lou Prescott, Special Events Manager
Larry Skinner, Facilities Manager
Lisa Blair, Gift Shop Manager
Lisa Davis, Director of Education
Camille Hunt, Collections Manager
Debra McStay, Special Events Coordinator
Shelly Garay, Administrative Assistant
Wendy Walton, Membership Coordinator

"SADDLE YOUR OWN HORSE"
Publication Staff

Editor– Karen Mullarkey
Designer – Michael T. Ricker
Photographer – Rhonda Hole
Photo Assistant - Camille Hunt
Writers – Terrell Lamb
           Bill Lawrence
           Jennifer Nielsen
           Dr. Herman Viola
Introduction – Reid Slaughter
Researchers – Kathy Jackson and Debra McStay
Printed by - Authentic Press

A SPECIAL COWGIRL THANK YOU TO THE FOLLOWING PEOPLE WHO HAVE CONTRIBUTED IN SO MANY WAYS TO THIS GREAT MUSEUM:

Susan Adams
American Audio Visual
Jim Arndt
BRC Imagination Arts
Martha Burr
Patti Colbert
Datum Engineering
Terrie Davis
Displays Unlimited
Freddie Dorn
Dunaway Associates
Enstrom Studios
Tres Falls
FMG Design, Inc.
Lisa Flood
City of Fort Worth
Fort Worth Convention & Visitors Bureau
Fort Worth Exposition and Livestock Show
Gideon Toal
Richard Haas
Chris Harmon
Amy Hoban
Rhonda Hole
Imagination Celebration
Kathy Jackson
JJT
Lawrence Johnson Productions
Duane H. King
Terrell Lamb
Bill Lawrence
Pam Lawrence
Brian Lebel
Mary Lou LeCompte
Linbeck Construction Corporation
Judy Logan
The Loomis Agency
Luskey/Ryons
Barbara Buhler Lynes
Maltbie Associates
Bill Manns
Sarah Massey
Milan Gallery
Montage Imagers
Karen Mullarkey - Photography Consultant
Pelton Marsh Kinsella
Pier One Photography Staff
Phoenix Graphics
PIXAR
John Pokrifcsak
B. Byron Price
Printing Plus
Michael T. Ricker
Glenda Riley
Joyce Roach
Margy Romans
Van Romans
Mary Schmitt
Pat Schutts
David M. Schwarz/Architectural Services, Inc.
Rufus Seder – Eye Think, Inc.
Ann Shelton
Joseph Sherwood & Linda Kohn
Thomas Sims
Southwest Solutions Group
Kenneth Springer
Rick Stewart
Summit Consultants
Sundance Projects Group
Jerry Thompson
Bill Thornton
Lillian Turner
Barbara Van Cleve
Dr. Herman Viola
Walt Disney Imagineering
West Office Exhibit Designs
Dr. Richard Scott White
Will Rogers Memorial Center

Credits

PHOTO CAPTIONS

Cover - Mamie Francis Hafley and her favorite horse, Napoleon
Back - cover Nancy Bragg Witmer
Inside front cover - Pauline Nesbitt
Inside back cover - Annie Oakley
p. 22 - Tillie Baldwin
p. 23 – top, Bonnie Gray; bottom, Kathy Daughn
p. 24 – Charmayne James and Scamper
p. 25 – top, Sissy Thurman; bottom, Sheri Cervi
p. 26 – top, clockwise from back left Tad Lucas, unknown, Ruth Roach, Vera McGinnis, Florence Hughes Randolph; bottom, Mamie Francis Hafley
p. 27 – top, Margie and Alice Greenough; center, Margie Roberts Hart; bottom, Nancy Kelley Sheppard
p. 28 – top, Rae Beach; bottom left, Bertha Blancett; bottom right, Alice Greenough Orr
p. 29 – top, Fern Sawyer; bottom, Jonnie Jonckowski
p. 31 – top, Thena Mae Farr and Nancy Binford
p. 32 – Kim Smith
p. 33 – top left, Tootie Hansen; top right, postcard; bottom, Amy and Elsie Cooksley
p. 34 – top left, Sara Guenzler; top right, Jeanne Dickinson; bottom, Shannon Kirby
p. 35 – top, KaDee Chew; bottom, Anna and Katy Whitlock
p. 36 – Bernice Dean
p. 37 – Millie Blache
p. 38 – top, Judy Golladay, Range Rider and Rodeo Grandma, Ellensburg, Washington; bottom left, Connie Bennett, Range Rider and Kay Shelton, Rancher, Ellensburg, Washington; bottom center, Horses – Ched in foreground and Cadillac Jack, Ellensburg, WA; Bottom right, Kay Shelton with Ched and Rodeo Jack
p. 39 – bottom, Reine Shelton; top, child from Lapp Ranch
p. 40 – Texas Guinan
p. 41 – Dale Evans
p. 43 – Judy Lynn
p. 44 – Gail and Terrie Davis
p. 45 – Reba McEntire

PHOTO CREDITS

Academy of Motion Picture Arts and Sciences, p. 40
Buffalo Bill Historical Center, Cody, Wyoming; Vincent Mercaldo Collection; P.71.356, inside back cover
Glenbow Archives, Calgary, Alberta, p. 37
Rhonda Hole, p. 10, 11, 12, 13, 14, 15, 16, 17, 18, 19, 20, 44
Library of Congress/LCUSZ c4-1008, p. 30
Courtesy Bill Manns, p. 47
Molly Morrow Photography, Ellensburg, Washington p. 38
Photofest, p. 45, 46
Courtesy The Roy Rogers and Dale Evans Museum, p. 41
Courtesy Kathleen Jo Ryan, www.kjryan.com, p. 32
John Schultz Photography, p. 43
Thomas Sims Archives, p. 43
Troy Smith, Sargent, Nebraska, p. 39
Courtesy Don Shugart, p. 23
Courtesy Kenneth Springer, p. 24
Courtesy © 1986 Barbara Van Cleve, p. 31
Courtesy © 1986 Barbara Van Cleve, p. 33
Courtesy © 2001 Barbara Van Cleve, p. 34
Courtesy © 1987 Barbara Van Cleve, p. 34
Courtesy © 1991 Barbara Van Cleve, p. 34
Courtesy © 2001 Barbara Van Cleve, p. 35
Courtesy © 2001 Barbara Van Cleve, p. 35

HONOREE PHOTOS COURTESY OF

Whitman Mission National Historic Site, National Park Service
Lynda A. Sanchez
Laura Ingalls Wilder Memorial Society, Inc.
Amon Carter Museum
Colorado State Historical Society
Panhandle-Plains Historical Museum
Kari Lanting
Michael J. Marten
Pixar Animation Studios
Theresa Montgomery
Montana Historical Society, Helena
Glenbow Archives Calgary, Alberta
Cappy Jackson
G. Provost
Glenn Ellman

QUOTATION CREDITS

p. 12, *A Queen Named King*, Mary Virginia Fox, Eakin Press, 1986.

p.25, *Cowgirls: Women of the American West*, Teresa Jordan, University of Nebraska Press, 1982.

p. 31, from *Standard of the West: The Justin Story*

p. 35, from *Voices & Visions of the American West*, Barney Nelson, Texas Monthly Press, 1986.

p. 36, from *I'll Gather My Geese*, Hallie Crawford Stillwell, Texas A&M University Press, © 1991.

p. 38, from *I'll Gather My Geese*, Hallie Crawford Stillwell, Texas A&M University Press, © 1991.

p. 37, Excerpts from NO LIFE FOR A LADY by Agnes Morley Cleaveland. Copyright 1941 by Agnes Morley Cleaveland; copyright renewed © 1969 by Loraine Lavendar. Reprinted by permission of Houghton Mifflin Company. All rights reserved.

p. 39, from *Frontier Children*, Linda Peavy and Ursula Smith, University of Oklahoma Press, 1999.

Page 52-53 : Richard Haas - mural study for the National Cowgirl Museum and Hall of Fame

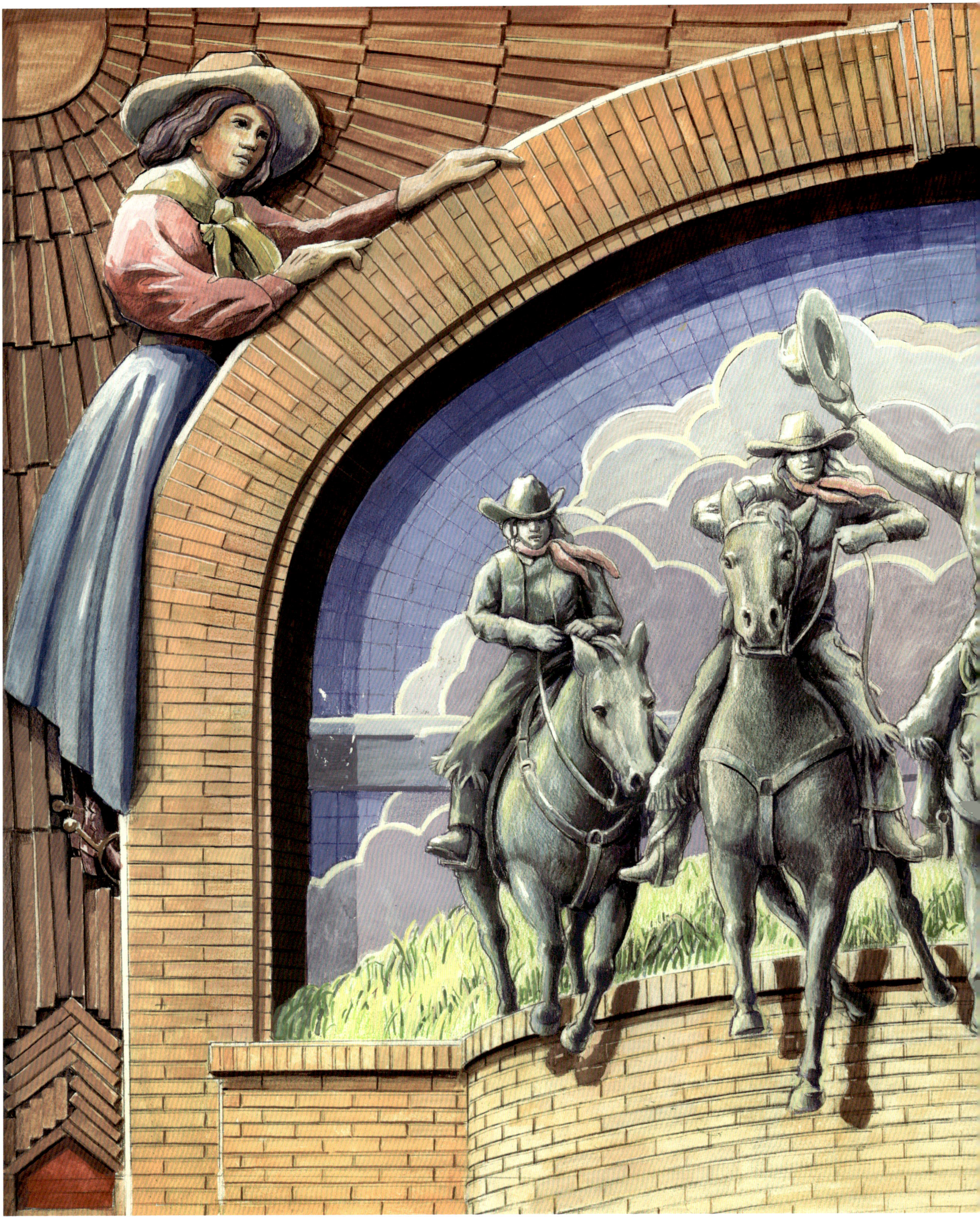

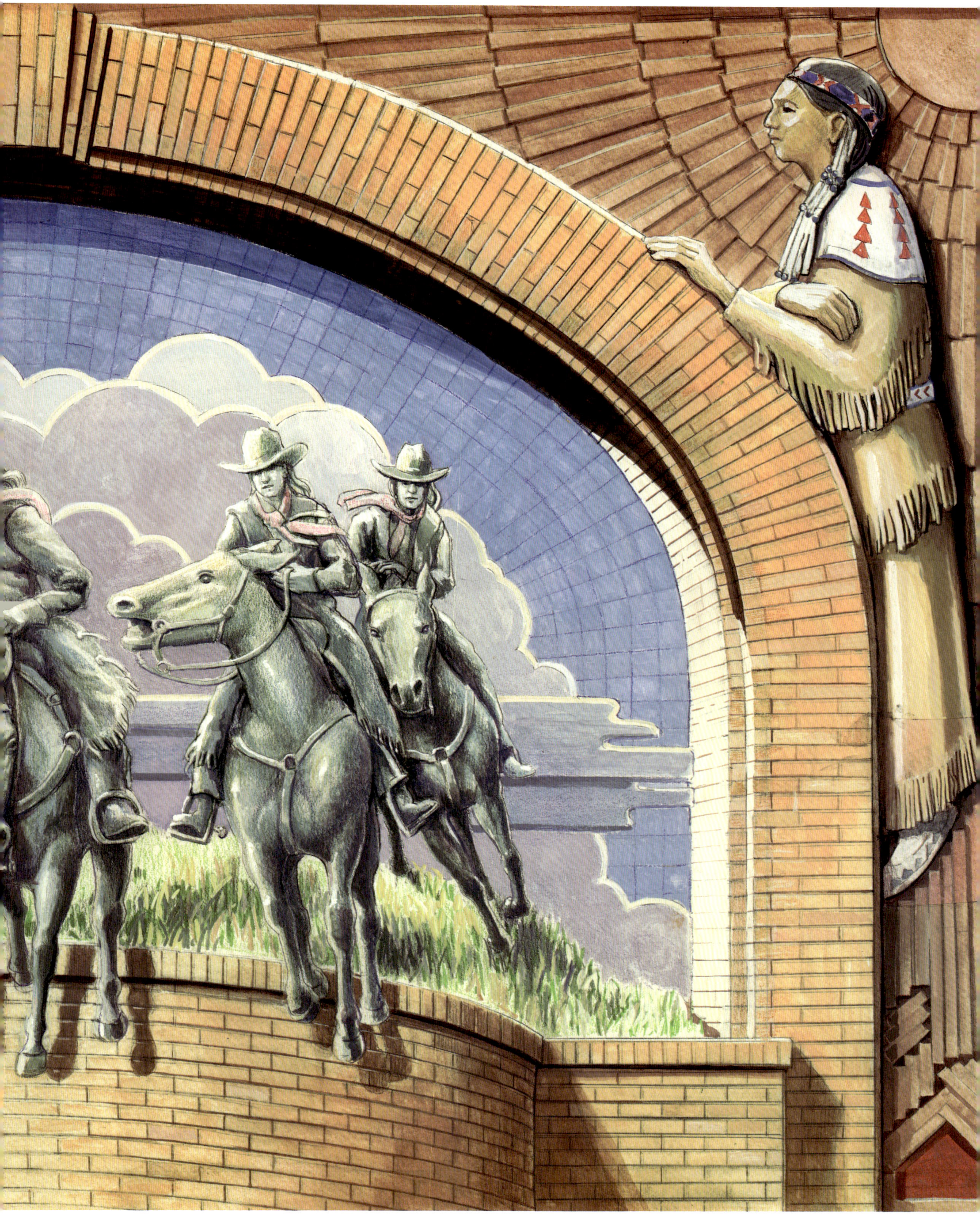

Honorees in the National Cowgirl Museum's Hall of Fame

Betty Kruse Accomazzo (1926-1989)
1983 The daughter of German immigrants, Betty made a significant contribution to the preservation of Western History with the publication of a five-volume anthology of stories told by pioneer families of Arizona. She was also a civic leader, serving with the 4-H, the National Livestock Show, the Arizona State Cowbelles and the community council. Betty was honored as *Arizona's Foremost Humanitarian*.

Anna Lee Aldred
1983 Anna, the daughter of a race horse-trainer, began riding at three and was racing ponies at six. By 12, she rode flat and relay races. She obtained her jockey's license at 18, making her the first woman jockey in the U.S. A fierce competitor, Anna retired from racing in 1944 and started a riding school in California. One year later, she began trick riding, performing in major rodeo shows throughout the western states.

Tillie Baldwin (1888-1958)
2000 Tillie was an all-around athlete when she emigrated to America from Norway and, inspired by seeing a cowgirl movie being filmed, learned trick riding. Soon working for Captain Baldwin's Wild West Show, she later joined Will Rogers' vaudeville troupe and then the 101 Ranch. She began to rodeo in 1912 and excelled at all rodeo events. Tillie was the first woman to win a roman race and possibly the first woman to try bulldogging.

Eve Ball (1890-1984)
1982 Eve wanted to be remembered for her work in oral history. Following a lifelong fascination with the West, she moved to New Mexico to learn the histories of the Anglo, Spanish and Apache. She impressed upon each group the importance of preserving their heritage and gained the confidence of many. Though she did not actually begin writing until age 60, her books and articles are such a significant contribution that many universities use them as reference textbooks for historical studies.

Mary Ellen "Dude" Barton
1984 Dude's life is characterized by her work on the family ranch and her rodeo successes. Many times competing against men in rodeo events, Dude proved that she could compete on equal terms with anybody and win. She served as the first vice-president of the GRA and promoted standardized rules and prize money. Dude purchased her old home farm from her parents and settled down to work the land settled by her grandparents.

"Texas" Rose Bascom (1922-1993)
1981 Rose was a professional trick roper, trick rider and movie actress. Known as the *Queen of the Trick Ropers*, she learned to ride and rope from Pearl Elder and, after marrying Weldon Bascom, spent thirteen years performing at rodeos. Her act took her to Hollywood where she performed on stage and in movies. She toured the world with USO shows. Her fluorescent trick roping act was billed as *The Most Beautiful Stage Performance in the World*.

Kathryn Binford (1888-1987)
1976 Kathryn moved to Texas from Illinois and married Gene Binford in 1910. Together, they forged a large ranch near Wildorado, stocking it with Hereford cattle, building fences, and farming a few acres. When Gene died in 1934, Kathryn raised their two daughters and managed the ranch alone, often driving wagons through the snow to feed cattle or riding out to mend fences. Despite the hardships, Kathryn became a successful rancher and an influential civic leader.

Nancy Binford (1921-1998)
1979 Nancy Binford, one of the country's premier horsewomen, won many horse shows, races, and cutting horse championships, but she will always be best remembered as co-producer, along with Thena Mae Farr, of the Tri-State All Girl Rodeos. Really *all-girl* from the contestants down to the judges, clowns and staff, they created opportunities for rodeo women not found in any other venue. Nancy also helped organize the fledgling GRA and served one term as president.

Faye Blackstone
1982 Faye taught herself to trick ride to break the boredom to and from school. At a local rodeo, Faye saw Mabel Strickland ride and thought, *that's what I want to do*. Much to the chagrin of her parents, she began riding in rodeos, eventually marrying Vick Blackstone, a Texas cowboy. Faye and Vick were rodeo stars for 13 years, with Faye creating new trick-riding maneuvers, including the Reverse Fender Drag, and eventually settled in Florida to ranch.

Reba Perry Blakely
1979 When she was a young child, Reba learned to ride a horse because she had difficulty walking. From that start, she became an accomplished trick roper, rider, and World Champion Relay Rider. She left rodeo to teach horsemanship, but with her interest in preserving rodeo history, Reba became a recognized historical researcher, using collected stories from the people she met and her own experiences to become an author of western and rodeo history.

Bertha Blancett (1883-1979)
1999 A pioneer in women's rodeo competition, Bertha was the first woman to ride broncs at Cheyenne, marking the start of women competing in rodeos. Making a name for herself as a bronc rider, she joined several wild west shows, including the 101 Ranch Show, where she married Del Blancett. Bertha moved to California where, with her husband, she worked in films under contract to Bison Pictures. Between movies, she competed at rodeo venues.

Faye Johnson Blesing (1920-1999)
1978 Faye started her career as a movie stuntwoman standing in for many female movie stars. She learned to trick ride and rope, putting together an act with her brothers, and went on the rodeo circuit. Headlining the Madison Square Garden Championship Rodeo for seven years, Faye, with her palomino, *Flash*, became a world-famous rodeo star dedicated to promoting the sport. She also appeared in rodeos and films with Gene Autry and Roy Rogers.

Eulalia "Sister" Bourne (c.1890-1984)
1996   Sister was a true Arizona pioneer. Overcoming tremendous hardships, she spent over 40 years teaching in rural one-room schools in southern Arizona. She homesteaded ranching property in the 1930s, doing all the work herself on weekends and teaching during the week. Sister published four books based on her life experiences. Sister was named 1973 Arizona Press Woman of the Year, honored by the Arizona Historical Society and named Outstanding Arizona Author.

Clara Brown (c.1800-1885)
1997   Born a slave in Virginia, Clara bought her own freedom when she was 57. One of the first African-Americans to come to Colorado, she became a property owner, leading activist and pillar of the community. Clara created Denver's first Sunday School and was instrumental in founding the St. James Methodist Church. Her home was always open to those in need and served as a hospital, hotel and refuge. She is venerated as a true pioneer in Colorado.

Lindy Burch
1997   Lindy holds the distinction of being the first woman to win the NCHA Futurity, and she set a record score while doing it. She was also the first female president of the NCHA. Lindy was raised riding horses but did not see her first cutting event until she was 14. Now a respected horse trainer and cutting champion, she promotes cutting internationally through clinics and competitions.

Mamie Sypert Burns (1895-1982)
1981   From 1942 until 1965, Mamie reigned as First Lady of the Pitchfork ranch, one of Texas' oldest and largest ranches. Raised in Houston under the tutelage of her aunts, she brought a new dimension to the ranch with her sophistication and expectations. Prepared more for high society than ranch life, marriage brought her to West Texas to make a home. Mamie was a gracious hostess and could perform any job, inside the house or out on the range.

Wanda Harper Bush
1978   The - 150 - year old Harper Ranch is home for Wanda. Here, like her ancestors, she raises livestock and trains horses. Instrumental in the organization of the GRA, Wanda has been one of its most awarded champions, winning thirty-three World Championships, including three All-Around titles. Curtailing rodeo activities, Wanda turned to raising horses and established herself as one of the premier horse trainers, garnering praise for both her horse skills and training clinics.

Elsa Spear Byron (1896-1992)
1990   Born in 1896 into one of Wyoming's first ranching families, Elsa acquired her first Brownie camera when she was 12. She began a career that spanned more than 80 years documenting a vanishing way of life with photographs of the lives of the Crow Indians, ranchers and the everyday life around her. Elsa was an eyewitness to the changes in the West as she worked on the family ranch and later as a mountain guide .

Evelyn Cameron (1868-1928)
2001   Evelyn captured the history and spirit of early Montana with over 1800 photographs and 35 volumes of diaries. The daughter of a wealthy English family, she turned away from a genteel lifestyle to adopt the life of a Montana rancher. To make ends meet she turned to photography. While selling the pictures helped her financially, her images of the rugged landscape, the cattle and ranching tasks with almost daily written notations preserve a true impression of American frontier life.

Willa Cather (1873-1947)
1986   Willa's sensitivity to her surroundings appeared repeatedly in her stories and books. Raised on the edge of the western frontier, she wrote with a passion and clarity based in her own knowledge of the stories of early Nebraska settlers. Willa was editor of a national magazine, author of best-selling novels and winner of the Pulitzer Prize and several honorary degrees. Her writings were the first to mark America's *Coming of Age* in literature.

Mildred Douglas Chrisman (1895-1983)
1988   Mildred left an east coast finishing school and went west to join the 101 Ranch Wild West show, beginning a colorful career that included winning the World Champion Girl Bronc Rider title twice and acting in silent movies with Tom Mix. A versatile performer, Mildred was skilled in trick-riding, trick-shooting and training performing animals. After retiring, Mildred became a nurse and eventually opened her own museum dedicated to her cowgirl life.

Bebe Mills Clements (1884-1989)
1984   Born into a pioneer ranching family, Bebe spent most of her life tending to ranch matters. Though she was an equal partner with her husband, she operated the ranch alone much of the time. Her ranching efforts set new standards in sheep ranching. Always wanting to be a musician and an artist Bebe taught herself to play piano and wrote dozens of published and recorded songs. She also taught herself oil painting techniques.

Patsy Cline (1932-1963)
1994   The first woman inducted into the Country Music Hall of Fame, Patsy had a voice and singing style that remains an influence on the music world. Inspired to learn to sing and dance by a Shirley Temple movie, Patsy made her radio debut at 10 and received national attention when she appeared on the Arthur Godfrey show singing *Walking After Midnight*. Her short but stellar career ended in a 1963 plane crash.

Margaret "Peg" Coe
1982   As chair of the Buffalo Bill Memorial Association Board, Peg engineered and guided to completion the Buffalo Bill Historical Center in Cody. She began a lifelong relationship with the Buffalo Bill Museum as a volunteer when her mother was secretary of the association and her father was editor of a weekly newspaper. After she married Henry Coe, she moved into a more active role for the Center and, upon Henry's death, oversaw a period of great growth as a board member.

Nel Sweeten Cooper (1898-1990)
1984   Nel came to Arizona looking for adventure. She married a rancher and homesteaded one of the largest Mohair goat ranches in the state. After her husband died, she successfully managed the ranch as the only woman goat rancher in Arizona, converting it to a cattle ranch just as the prices for mohair began to fall. A pioneer and community leader, she recorded the hardships of ranching life in books and articles, including an autobiography.

Jewel Duncan (1902-1984)
1976   Jewel grew up on a West Texas ranch, learning to rope as part of the work. She began to rope against men in local contests becoming, the first woman to compete at the Pecos rodeo in 1929, and was rodeo queen there in 1935. Jewel, with her friend Isora DeRacy Young promoted themselves as the only two cowgirl calf ropers in the world competing against cowboys at a time when there were no women's roping contests.

Gene Krieg Creed (1909-1993)
1982   Gene became the youngest woman ever to win the bronc riding at Cheyenne in 1925. She and her sister Vaughn learned to ride before they were five and were soon helping their brothers break wild horses and pursue stray cattle on the family's Colorado ranch. One of the best cowgirls around, Gene won trick riding, relay races and bronc riding championships in a career spanning three decades and three continents.

Dale Evans (1912-2001)
1995   Beginning her career in show business singing for a Memphis radio station, Dale (born Francis Smith) made her way to Chicago where she was discovered by Paramount scouts. She came to Hollywood, working in films with John Wayne, Joe E. Brown and Roy Rogers, whom she married. Together with Roy, she made 27 films, a television series and raised a large family. Dale was named Texas Woman of the Year and California Mother of the Year.

Linda Mitchell Davis
1995   A fourth-generation rancher, Linda grew up in the drought of the early 1930s on the family ranch in New Mexico, learning ranching firsthand as a ranchhand. Linda attended Cornell to study agricultural economics, returning home to run the ranch. She married and moved to the CS Ranch she runs today. Her commitment to ranching and cattle raising brought her such awards as the Cattleman of the Year Award and the Golden Spur Award.

Thena Mae Farr (1927-1985)
1985   Thena Mae used the ranching skills she learned growing up to compete in every rodeo event from barrel racing to bronc riding. But her real fame came as she, along with her partner Nancy Binford, made history with their creation of the 1947 Tri-State All Girl Rodeo. A pioneer of women's professional rodeo, Thena Mae served as president of the GRA before retiring to the family ranch where she received recognition for ranching and community service.

Bernice Dean (1915-1980)
1986   Bernice was one of the most versatile Wild West and Rodeo performers. Her act included singing and dancing, trick riding, trick shooting, knife throwing, tricks with Mexican maguey ropes and bull whips, juggling, and a balancing trick on the rolling globe. She and her husband worked as an exhibition team for 45 years in every state and thirteen countries. Billed in Wild West shows, rodeos, circuses, motion pictures and television, Bernice earned worldwide acclaim.

Flaxie Fletcher (1911-2002)
1983   Though she was never a performer, Flaxie spent her life in rodeo. She worked outside the arena performing the behind the scenes jobs of arena secretary, timer or administrative assistant for some of the biggest rodeos. After leaving the rodeo circuit, Flaxie spent ten years as the executive secretary of the Rodeo Division at the National Cowboy Hall of Fame. She founded the Rodeo Historical Society and documented rodeo history through newsletters and publications.

Angie Debo (1890-1988)
1985   Angie set out to be a history teacher. Growing up in the Oklahoma frontier, she was a child who loved books and learning. Her dreams of teaching college history were blocked by a discrimination by most colleges against hiring women. She turned to writing about history as an alternate avenue. Priding herself on unyielding accuracy, her historical publications garnered her national acclaim, earning her the title, *First Lady of Oklahoma History.*

Margaret Formby
1994   Margaret took over leadership of the newly formed National Cowgirl Hall of Fame in 1976, expanding the Hall's focus to honor all western women and changing the name of the center to the National Cowgirl Hall of Fame and Western Heritage Center. Raised on a West Texas ranch, *growing up western*, as she called it, Margaret believed women should be recognized for their influence in western culture. With her involvement, the Hall expanded and received national recognition.

Grace Ingalls Dow (1877-1941)
1984   The youngest of the Ingalls children, Grace went to school in DeSmet. She eventually married a local farmer, Nathan Dow. With her husband's health failing, Grace and he rented out the farm and toured the Pacific Coast. Returning to DeSmet, Grace wrote neighborhood news items for the newspaper and cared for her sister Mary after their mother died. Upon Mary's death, Grace and her husband moved to Manchester.

Jimmie Gibbs-Munroe
1992   Born into the heritage of the 101 Ranch, Jimmie entered her first horse show at three, her first rodeo at ten, and had a rodeo career that included 11 NFR trips and becoming one of the top women in barrel racing. Jimmie served as the GRA/WPRA president for fourteen years, where, under her leadership, significant advances were made. She advanced the use of electronic timers at barrel races and was instrumental in women receiving equal prize money to men in rodeo events.

Laura Gilpin (1891-1979)
1987   Receiving her first camera when she was 12, Laura photographed the Southwest for more than 60 years. Working alone, Laura's works are unique because she pursued landscape photography, a field pioneered and traditionally practiced by men. Compelled not by scientific curiosity but by humane concerns, her interest in the land was as an environment that shaped human activity. Her four books, and thousands of photographs documented the relationships between people and the land.

Ruby Gobble
1982   Ruby can be described in many terms; accomplished horsewoman, trick rider, roping champion, rodeo queen, movie actress or ranch foreman. Raised on her family's Arizona ranch, she learned to ride at 3 on burros and mastered roping not long after. Beginning her rodeo career as a trick rider, Ruby switched to roping competitions, soon winning numerous awards and championships. Always a capable ranchhand, Ruby makes use of her versatile talents as foreman of the Chase Ranch in New Mexico.

Mary Ann "Molly" Goodnight (1839-1926)
1991   Wife of cattleman Charles Goodnight, Molly drove supply wagons and took charge of ranch operations when her husband was absent. Affectionately called *the little mother of the plains*, she cared for the cowhands and Indians who came to the ranch as a way to combat the loneliness of being the only woman in the area. Molly and her husband built Goodnight College, helped build a community church and were responsible for the preservation of Texas buffalo.

Marie Keen Gress (1914-2001)
1997   For more than 16 years during the 1930's and 1940s, Marie crisscrossed the country as a trick rider, steer wrestler, bronc rider, and performer in rodeos, circuses and wild west shows. She began her career as a trick rider with the 101 Ranch Show at 15. An innovative rider, she soon became a rodeo star, receiving billing with Gene Autry, Tad Lucas and Alice Sisty. Marie is considered a trailblazer for women in the steer wrestling event.

Helen Groves
1998   Raised on the legendary King Ranch, it seemed natural for Helen to become an ambassador for the equine industry. Over the years she has become known as the *first lady of cutting*, spending more than two decades breeding, raising and riding cutting horses on her ranch while competing at almost every major show. Helen has also established herself as a major presence in breeding and racing Thoroughbreds and a leading supporter of equine research.

"Mamie" Francis Hafley (1886-1950)
1981   Mamie thrilled audiences with her daredevil act of riding her horse off a 50-foot-high platform into a barrel of water just 10 feet across. Between 1908 and 1917, she performed this stunt 628 times. She also performed as a sharpshooter, before and after the years of her diving act. Learning to shoot when she was a child, Mamie did her rifle shooting from horseback, performing in vaudeville and the wild west shows.

Margaret Pease Harper (1911-1991)
1981   Margaret founded the Texas Panhandle Heritage Foundation and was the driving force behind the creation of the musical drama, *Texas*, performed each year against the backdrop of Palo Duro Canyon. A Minnesota native, she came to Texas by way of teaching assignments in Arizona and Peru. This teacher turned author and playwright also co-founded the Lone Star Ballet. Margaret maintained that the arts are an important part of society and should be shared by everyone.

Bonnie Gray Harris (1891-1988)
1981   Tall and athletic, Bonnie is best remembered for her amazing stunts and trick-riding. Allegedly the first woman to perform the *under-the-belly crawl* on a horse, she also jumped her horse over an open car with passengers and was one of the first women to ride bulls in Mexican bullfights. As the movie industry flourished in California, so did Bonnie's career as a stunt rider doubling for most of the stars of the time.

Margie Roberts Hart (1916-1982)
1987   One of the top women bronc riders from the 1930s through the 1950s, Margie broke horses for her father and neighbors while still in grade school. Her ability to ride rough stock led to winning the Ladies Bronc Riding Championship at Cheyenne in 1941 and a career as a trick rider. Retiring from rodeo, Margie worked with horses much of the rest of her life. She was also an accomplished artist.

Margie Greenough Henson
1978   Margie began her rodeo career in 1929 with Jack King's Wild West Rodeo. Growing up on a working ranch where Margie and her seven siblings learned to ride and rope as part of the daily chores, she became a champion bronc rider. Known as one of the *Riding Greenoughs*, Margie went on to rodeo and ride exhibitions in almost every state and for almost every big rodeo, usually being the only female bronc rider.

Alice Adams Holden (1907-1994)
1983   Once riding 27 broncs in one day, she was billed as the girl who could ride anything on four feet. Alice, riding since the age of five, had a rodeo career spanning 30 years and included bronc riding championships in the U.S. and Cuba. Retiring from event participation, she served in administrative roles for rodeos until leaving to run a ranch with her husband. She later became an accomplished organist and worked for the Oklahoma Democratic party.

Juanita Hackett Howell (1910-2001)
1986   Juanita, whose trick riding and trick roping brought her fame throughout the U.S., did not see a rodeo until the age of 20, when she joined her mother in the King Brothers Show and learned the life of a wild west performer. Meeting and marrying her husband in the rodeo arena, she performed with him as a top trick act for over 20 years. Juanita was also one of the original Cowboy Turtle Association members.

Stella Cox Hughes
1988   Stella spent most of her life on horseback, either competing in rodeo and show events, or as a working cowgirl. She taught horsemanship clinics for young girls. She related much of her knowledge about horses and ranch life in hundreds of published articles and short stories, receiving the Golden Spur Award. Stella's cooking skills gained attention from annual cattle drives, resulting in the publication of *Chuck Wagon Cooking*. Stella also organized annual trail rides for women.

Sabra Lee Humphrey
1981   Sabra's artistic talent captures the history of the West and ranching on canvas using knowledge acquired growing up on a southwestern New Mexico ranch. Her early critics were the cowboys and oldtimers who intimately knew the West and the animals in it. In her early years, she was discouraged from painting western art in lieu of more modern subjects. Through her desire to paint it *right*, Sabra's artworks are accurate portrayals of western life.

Vaughn Krieg Huskey   (1904-1976)
1989   Vaughn started her rodeo career in 1926 as a trick rider to fill in for her sister, Gene. She became one of the top bronc riders and one of the first women to bulldog a steer from a moving car. In the 1930's, Vaughn was one of the few women producers in rodeo, even putting on a 1942 event at the Paris, Texas, fairgrounds that was one of the first all girl-rodeos.

Caroline Quiner Ingalls   (1839-1924)
1984   Matriarch of the Ingalls family, Caroline, although born and raised on the frontier, was an educated and cultured woman. Quiet and gentle, she had five children and was known for her kindness and concern for others. With her husband, she moved to Kansas, then Minnesota where she lost her only son. After spending two years in Iowa, Caroline moved to the Dakota Territory becoming without knowing it, the first settlers of De Smet.

Mary Ingalls   (1865-1928)
1984   Eldest of the Ingalls children, Mary dreamed of becoming a school teacher until she was stricken with scarlet fever and lost her sight. She instead attended the Iowa State College for the Blind, graduating with high marks. Returning home, she lived with her mother and wove colorful *fly nets* for horses. She was a church organist and Sunday school teacher.

Charmayne James
1992   With her horse, Scamper, Charmayne set an unprecedented record by winning the World Championship Barrel Racing title ten consecutive years. She was also the first barrel racer in rodeo history to win more money than any PRCA cowboy during a single rodeo season. Charmayne began barrel racing in New Mexico as a young girl, entering the ProRodeo circuit at 14. Charmayne trains her own horses for barrel racing, cutting and team roping competitions.

Jonnie Jonckowski
1991   Jonnie's competitive spirit helped her overcome many barriers to become a two-time world champion bull rider, but she also eliminated these same barriers for the women who followed her. Many arenas began to allow women to ride rough stock for the first time since the 1930s. An athlete her entire life, Jonnie tried bull riding for fun. She found the sport could give her the challenge she desired.

Suzanne Norton Jones
1999   Suzanne is one of the most influential trainers, breeders and judges in the equestrian world. The daughter of an army cavalryman, she began showing horses at age four. Her career included winning virtually every major horse show in North America and becoming one of the top Quarter horse breeders. Suzanne acquired judging cards in several breed associations and served on the AQHA International Committee. She is also an author and columnist for a major horse journal.

Martha Josey
1985   Recognized as a leading barrel racing authority, Martha has dedicated herself to improving the equine industry and the sport of barrel racing. As a young girl with a natural athletic ability and a love for horses, it was a logical step for Martha to compete in rodeo events. After years of winning, she began to teach others horsemanship and barrel racing. Her clinics have motivated barrel racers at all levels for decades.

Enid Justin   (1894-1990)
1978   Enid was the daughter of legendary boot maker H.J. Justin. When her father died and Justin Boot Company moved to Fort Worth, she decided to remain in her hometown and start her own boot shop. Using the skills and knowledge she learned working for her father, Enid founded Nocona Boot Company. Her work was not only in the business world. Enid was a well regarded humanitarian, civic leader and generous supporter of her community.

Kathy Kennedy   (1956-1981)
1984   Like her father and grandfather, Kathy was a roper. From early childhood, she dreamed of becoming the world's best woman roper. Kathy won her first rodeo event, team roping, at 14 and was the only female competitor. She won her first world title in 1977. Before her career was cut short by cancer, Kathy became a major competitor in the professional ranks of the GRA, where she worked all the roping events.

Henrietta King   (1832-1925)
1982   Henrietta, the daughter of a Presbyterian minister, married Richard King, the founder of the King Ranch. As the ranch matriarch, she was known for her hospitality and compassion, extending help to the needy and sick. Henrietta literally created the town of Kingsville by donating the land. When ""Captain"" King died, Henrietta became the sole owner and manager of the world's largest ranch. She ultimately created an empire of over a million acres.

Sheila Kirkpatrick
1992   Sheila makes custom cowboy hats the same way hatmakers did a century ago. Using antique tools and methods, she hand shapes each hat. Growing up as the daughter of a rodeo announcer, Sheila saw a lot of rodeos and cowboys, and their hats. With her accumulated knowledge and an interest in hats that goes back to her childhood, she preserves a bit of the old West each time she turns a out a new hat.

Nita Brooks Lewallen
1997   Nita embraced the ranching life she grew up in. Even as a contender in the rodeo circuit, her main interests remained ranching and horses. Nita dedicated over half a century exploring the horse industry, particularly thoroughbred breeding, and her contributions have been significant. She was named the Texas Breeder of the Year three years running and became the first woman to receive the USDA and Goodyear awards for Rancher of the year.

Bobby Brooks Kramer
2000   For the last six decades, Bobby has been recognized for her outstanding contributions to the horse industry in Montana. Riding since she was three, Bobby has carried on the ranching traditions of her parents and grandparents. She and her husband formed the Hanging Diamond A horse ranch after both pursued notable rodeo careers. Bobby still produces award-winning horses in cutting, trail, reining, and pleasure riding.

Ann Lewis   (1958-1968)
1981   In 1968, Ann was the youngest Barrel Racing Champion in WPRA history. Ann began running barrels before she started kindergarten, placing in her first open when she was 5. Ann and her twin sister got their first barrel horse when they were 7. When Ann was 8, she was one of the youngest IPRA members and consistently outran more experienced racers. Called *Annie the Okie,* she held such a substantial lead in competition that when a car accident ended her career, she won the GRA barrel racing championship posthumously.

Julie Krone
1999   Since her earliest tomboy days, Julie knew what she wanted. Nothing but racing kept her interest. She began her career exercising horses at Churchill Downs and was racing in a year. Eventually earning over $80 million in purses, Julie made more than 3,500 trips to the winner's circle. She retired as the top female jockey in the history of horse racing. After racing, Julie turned to work in television broadcasting as a race analyst.

Rebecca Tyler Lockhart
2000   Rebecca learned about horses from the cowboys she grew up around. Called by many a natural-born horseperson, she spent more time with horses than at school. Rebecca gained an enviable reputation as a breeder of fine horses. Founder of the American Paint Stock Horse Association, precursor to the American Paint Horse Association, she began a movement that made the Paint into one of the fastest growing breeds in the world.

Flores LaDue   (1883-1951)
2001   The only cowgirl to claim three world championships for trick and fancy roping, Flores was undefeated in that event. Growing up on a Sioux reservation, she began her career with a wild west show and there met her husband, Guy Weadick. Together, they organized and produced the first Calgary Stampede along with operating a dude ranch and producing smaller rodeos. Flores is reputed to have been the first trick roper to perform the trick known as the Texas Skip.

Tad Lucas   (1902-1990)
1978   For a decade, Tad was known as the world's best female rodeo performer. In her career, she collected all of the major trophies and titles available to rodeo cowgirls, though she achieved her greatest fame as a fearless and innovative trick rider. Tad, the youngest of 24 children, made her professional debut in 1917. She moved to Ft. Worth soon after and began touring with Wild West shows. She first competed in trick riding in England.

Rose Wilder Lane   (1886-1968)
1984   The daughter of Laura Wilder, Rose was a gifted child academically. She left home at 17 to work for Western Union, then began a successful, but short-lived real estate career. Rose began her writing career as a feature writer for the San Francisco Bulletin. Leaving that job to work for the Red Cross, Rose traveled the world and wrote of her adventures, gaining national attention. She served as mentor and patron of her mother's works.

Goldia Malone   (1903-1999)
1981   Goldia became a world famous trick rider after seeing her first Wild West show at 17. She made a deal with Curly Griffith to teach her trick riding in exchange for exercising horses. Soon performing in local fairs, Goldia was discovered and hired for contract work trick riding and bronc riding with the Malone Wild West Show. An accident caused Goldia to retire to farming, where she won many awards for innovative and experimental practices.

Harriet "Bita" Lee   (1928-1991)
1996   Born a twin on the 300,000 acres of the Fernandez ranch, Bita grew up with the Spanish and Navajo, not speaking English until she was six. She attended the University of New Mexico, returning to the ranch when her father took ill. Bita was an expert horsewoman, a renowned heel roper, cook and hard working ranchhand. She successfully managed the ranch for nearly 30 years, implementing breeding improvements and designing new facilities for working cattle.

Wilma Mankiller
1994   Wilma became the first female principal chief in the history of the Cherokee people. Born in Oklahoma, her family moved to California as part of the BIA Relocation Program. Returning to Oklahoma, Wilma worked to educate and empower the Cherokee Nation and, through community development, to preserve its heritage. She led the Nation to become more self-sustaining and less dependent on federal programs, which gained them greater independence and strengthened tribal institutions.

Maria Martinez (1887-1980)
1998 Maria, the most famous of Pueblo Indian potters, along her husband revived the ancient pueblo craft of pottery making after discovering the process used in crafting San Ildefonso prehistorical pueblo pottery. Using the knowledge of pottery making she learned as a child, Maria reintroduced the world to the highly polished black vessels. Her ceramics quickly became valued artworks and are exhibited in museums worldwide.

Bernice McLaughlin (1891-1985)
1977 Born in Canada in 1891, Bernice won the Canadian Rodeo Champion High Jump contest in 1911, setting a new record, on a borrowed cowpony. She was a natural horsewoman, winning numerous jumping contests and relay races. Raised working a ranch, she and her husband homesteaded in New Mexico, and upon his death, Bernice managed to keep the ranch, despite challenges to her citizenship status, and increase its size and success.

Louise Massey (1902-1983)
1982 Louise grew up on a ranch but was raised to be a musician. Along with her two brothers and husband, she performed as Louise and The Westerners, becoming stars on NBC for 19 years until retiring. Louise wrote *White Azaleas*, which sold 3 million copies, and *My Adobe Hacienda*, listed simultaneously on the Lucky Strike Hit Parade and the Hillbilly Hit Parade. She was admitted into the Smithsonian Institution Broadcaster's Library in 1976.

Marlene Eddleman McRae
1995 A world champion barrel racer, Marlene has been riding or showing horses since she was six. Inspired by Dale Evans, she wanted to be a cowgirl and ride horses. Entering her first Little Britches rodeo, she began a string of championships that includes two gold medals from the 1988 Winter Olympics. A talented musician, Marlene decided in college to turn all her energies to rodeo competition. She continues her involvement with riding clinics and endorsements.

Sallie Reynolds Matthews (1861-1938)
1982 Sallie endured the hardships of pioneer life living in the isolation of cattle ranches. Though her formal education was limited to the sporadic presence of country school teachers, Sallie wrote *Interwoven: A Pioneer Chronicle*, a clan story of the experiences and complex relationships that developed between two families as they built a new country. Intended as a family history for the children, it has become a basic source of information on the history of the Texas frontier.

Augusta Metcalfe (1881-1971)
1983 A child of the true West, Augusta became recognized as one of the greatest Western painters. Raised on a homestead in ""No Man's Land"" in Oklahoma Indian Territory, she never attended a school and never had an art lesson. In 1911, Augusta won first prize in the State Fair for a painting, beginning a long string of awards and accolades for her work. She was a pioneer who recorded life of the early West as vividly as any writer.

Gertrude Maxwell (1908-1998)
1993 Gertrude's parents taught her to be self-sufficient. She spent forty years as a teacher and another thirty years as a hunting outfitter. This was in addition to running a ranch, training and breeding horses and dogs and farming. Her dream of attending medical school vanished in the Depression, so she turned to teaching, even starting a school where one was needed. Gertrude became interested in recording history and became a published author.

Pam Minick
2000 *Atomic Blonde* is how Pam's Las Vegas birth announcements read. Always competitive, her spirit and dedication made her a true ambassador for rodeo as a competitor and a promoter. Her list of accomplishments includes champion calf roper, actress, movie stuntperson, businesswoman and sports commentator. She served as Vice President of the WPRA and helped bring about significant advances for women's rodeo. Her popularity as a rodeo commentator helped increase interest in the sport as a whole.

Billie Hinson McBride
1981 Billie set a then unprecedented record by winning the title of World Champion GRA Barrel Racer for four consecutive years beginning in 1955. She and her sister began barrel racing after seeing a barrel race in the 1930s. The two competed together riding the same mare, usually claiming first and second place in the Texas rodeos. A GRA charter member, Billie served over thirteen years in different administrative roles, including Barrel Racing Director.

Lilla Day Monroe (1858-1929)
1982 Lilla began life as the daughter of an Indiana mill owner. Beginning as a schoolteacher, she became the first woman to practice before the Kansas Supreme Court. Lilla was a political activist who lobbied successfully for the Suffrage Amendment. She founded two journals and promoted progressive welfare, labor and property rights, minimum-wage standards, improved working conditions, child-hygiene regulations and state primaries. In her later years, she chronicled the history of Kansas pioneer women.

Vera McGinnis (1895-1990)
1979 Unlike many of her peers, Vera was not born on a ranch, but her athletic ability made her a natural when she discovered the rodeo. Beginning her career as an impromptu relay rider, she soon added trick riding, bronc and bull riding and Roman racing, winning at all events. A celebrated rider, Vera's most famous trick was the under-the-belly crawl at full speed. Touring with rodeo shows, she performed in Canada, Europe, Asia and the U.S.

Dixie Reger Mosely
1982 Youngest in a family of rodeo performers, Dixie made her trick riding debut at 5. She became the first juvenile professional rodeo clown while working Wild West shows. Primarily a trick rider, Dixie successfully competed in all rodeo events, though her best event was calf roping. She also raised and trained Quarter Horses for competition. Dixie was a charter member of the GRA and worked as contract representative promoting the rodeos.

Patsy Montana (1912-1996)
1987   Patsy was the first woman to sell a million records with *I Want To Be A Cowboy's Sweetheart*. The eleventh child, and the first daughter of an Arkansas farmer, Patsy learned to yodel and play the organ, guitar and violin. Beginning her career in radio in California, she worked rodeos and country programs with the Prairie Ramblers and the Sons of the Pioneers. She wrote more than 200 songs and was recognized worldwide.

Shelly Burmeister Mowery
1990   An active promoter of rodeo, Shelly has participated in the sport as a performer, rodeo queen and announcer with all the major TV networks. Also a rodeo consultant and an actress, Shelly served on the board of the National Cutting Horse Association and trains cutting horses with her husband. Using her celebrity, Shelly brought significant attention to the issues of raising the pay for rodeo events and equal pay for men and women in the major rodeos.

Lucille Mulhall (1885-1940)
1977   Called *the world's first cowgirl* by Will Rogers, Lucille was the best known western performer of her era. Learning to ride and rope on the family's Oklahoma ranch, she began her career performing in her father's Wild West show and became one of the earliest and most accomplished riding and roping champions. Competing with, and frequently beating male competitors in steer roping events, Lucille helped make women an integral part of rodeo.

Mattie Goff Newcombe
1994   Mattie was a pioneer in the sport of rodeo, raising the status of performers through her own rodeo contracts. She was a daring trick rider known for her speed and for never losing her hat. Mattie was a bronc rider that was never thrown and a relay rider who was never outrun. She was one of the first inductees into the National Cowboy Hall of Fame. After marrying, Mattie turned her attentions to her ranch in South Dakota.

Annie Oakley (1860-1926)
1984   Annie Oakley became an international legend in her own lifetime based on her shooting skills. Born into poverty in Ohio, Annie taught herself to shoot to help feed her family. A shooting contest against future husband Frank Butler started her on the road to stardom. In 1885, she joined the Buffalo Bill's Wild West Show as the only female performer. She traveled the world as the World's Champion Markswoman, hosting shooting clinics and performing onstage.

Georgia O'Keeffe (1887-1986)
1991   Born in rural Wisconsin, Georgia worked as a commercial artist and an art teacher as she developed a personal style of stripping her subjects to their purest forms and colors. Reaching the status of a national treasure, she was famous for the expressive power of light and the patterns of nature in her close-up paintings of flowers and landscapes. Splitting her time between New York and New Mexico, Georgia painted almost nine hundred works in her career.

Alice Greenough Orr (1902-1995)
1975   Growing up on a working ranch, Alice's rodeo life began with Jack King's Wild West Show riding saddle broncs, though she also did trick riding and occasionally rode bulls. Alice became an international rodeo star, performing in 46 states, Canada, Mexico, Spain, France, England, and Australia and winning four World Champion Saddle Bronc Rider titles. One of the *Riding Greenoughs*, Alice formed her own rodeo business and featured the first women's barrel racing events.

Ollie Osborn (1896-1989)
1982   Ollie was the first woman to pursue the sport of rodeo full time and be a constant champion. Born to Oregon homestead ranchers, she began competing in the early relay races when she was a teenager. But she discovered bronc riding and made a name for herself by riding *slick*, without hobbles, like the men. Remembered for her daring rides and extravagant tailor-made clothes, she continued to ride until 1932.

Margaret Owens (1922-1955)
1976   Margaret helped found the GRA and served as the organization's first president. Living on a ranch her entire life, she was an excellent horsewoman who rode in rodeos at a time when there were no events for women. Many times she would compete in match roping events after a show. A champion roper, she was among the first women to compete in roping at Pecos, Texas. Margaret actively promoted rodeo, helping with amateur and professional all girl rodeos.

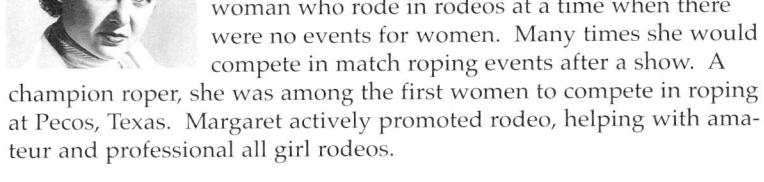

Mother Joseph Esther Pariseau (1823-1902)
1981   Esther made monumental contributions to health care, education, and social works throughout the Northwest. The daughter of a French-Canadian carriage maker, she joined the Sisters of Providence and was sent to Fort Vancouver to oversee construction of a convent and schoolhouse. As the architect, construction supervisor, and chief fund raiser, she built 9 schools, 15 hospitals and a mission, becoming the first to provide care for the orphans, elderly and mentally ill in Washington Territory.

Cynthia Ann Parker (1827-1864)
1998   Cynthia was captured when she was nine years old during a Comanche raid on Fort Parker in 1836, and grew up as an adopted Comanche, eventually marrying a war leader. Twenty-four years later, she was "rescued", but could not re-adjust to life within white culture. While with the Comanche, Cynthia had three children, one of whom was the great Comanche chief, Quanah Parker. Though she never re-adjusted to the white world, Cynthia is an inspiration for survival.

Mary Parks (1910-1997)
1979   Mary began riding when she was big enough to sit in the saddle. She and her mother broke horses on their Colorado ranch, while her father ran a mercantile in town. She began riding in local rodeos, soon leaving the ranch to begin a career as a celebrated saddle bronc rider. She married Bill Parks and crisscrossed the continent, competing in rodeos in every state, Mexico, Canada and Cuba. Retiring in 1948, Mary continued to ride in quadrilles and barrel race.

Hildred Goodwine Phillips (1918-1998)
1989   Hildred was successful as a Western painter and sculptor because her subjects have always been the horses she knew and loved. Her great love of horses began in childhood on a farm in Michigan where she studied each detail of the teams of workhorses used in everyday chores. When she began to paint and sculpt, Hildred relied on her knowledge of horses to create thousands of artworks depicting life in the West.

Lucyle Garner Richards (1909-1995)
1987   Leaving her family ranch in Talihena, Oklahoma, Lucyle toured the country as a saddle bronc rider. She performed around the world, tagged by the press *the prettiest and best dressed cowgirl in America.* She bought her own plane and learned acrobatic flying in 1939. As a member of the Women Airforce Service Pilots, Lucyle was able to make major contributions to the Allies by flying bombers between the U.S. and Britain.

Sue Pirtle
1981   Called *the most versatile cowgirl in the history of the GRA*, Sue won 11 World titles as All-Around Cowgirl, calf roper, ribbon roper, bareback rider and bull rider. Sue actively promoted the image of the modern cowgirl through television, documentaries, sports competitions and movie appearances. Dedicated to promoting the image of the women's rodeo, she served on the board of directors of the WPRA and as a director of the GRA.

Mitzi Lucas Riley
1996   The daughter of Tad Lucas, Mitzi was born into rodeo. Learning to ride before she could walk, Mitzi made her debut at six, filling in for her injured mother in a trick-riding act. A daring rider, she routinely turned down offers from Hollywood, while performing in rodeos coast to coast for twenty years. Retired from rodeo, Mitzi served on the board of the Rodeo Historical Society, establishing the Tad Lucas Award to recognize outstanding women in rodeo.

Florence Hughes Randolph (c.1898-1971)
1994   Ten time World Champion Cowgirl Trick Rider and World Champion Bronc Rider Florence made more than 500 rodeo appearances - bronc riding, trick roping, trick riding and roman riding. A petite woman, Florence was 13 before she learned to ride a horse and taught herself stunt riding. She worked in wild west shows, raced motorcycles, doubled for movie stars and produced her own show, *Princess Mohawk's Wild West Hippodrome*.

Ruth Roach (1896-1986)
1989   Ruth ran away from home to join the 101 Ranch Wild West Show as a trick rider. Her contest debut came at the 1917 Fort Worth Roundup, America's first indoor rodeo, as a bronc rider. Dubbed the *soft-spoken, rough-riding golden girl of the West,* she wore trademark giant hair bows and boots hand-tooled with hearts. She is remembered for trick riding up the steps, across the lobby and through the dining room of Fort Worth's Texas Hotel.

Betty Gayle Cooper Ratliff (1952-1999)
1987   Born into a family of rodeo stars, Betty established herself as one of the top calf-roping champions. Growing up on a ranch near Hobbs, New Mexico, Betty won her first championship at 12 in Junior Calf Roping. A diligent rodeo supporter, she helped reorganize the American Junior Rodeo Association and worked as rodeo director of the WPRA to strengthen the sport. She coached the men's and women's rodeo teams for Southeastern Oklahoma State University to national titles.

Carol Rose
2001   One of the first females to become a leader in the equine industry, Carol began competing in horse events as a child. She inherited her passion for horses from her mother, who taught her to ride and care for them as a basis for *life lessons*. A world champion in non-pro cutting horse competition, Carol has evolved into one of the world's leading breeders and exhibitors of Quarter Horses, dedicated to making a positive difference.

Pamela Harr Rattey
1981   Pamela grew up in California and began sculpting to use as therapy with handicapped children. After learning bronze casting, she combined it with her love of history and her own personal experiences of ranch work to create bronzes of stories and characters of the West. A member of Women Artists of the American West, Pamela exhibits her work throughout the country. Pamela and her husband Harvey Rattey, manage their own gallery and foundry in Montana.

Sacajawea
1977   A Shoshone Indian, Sacajawea was the only woman to accompany the 1802-06 Lewis and Clark expedition into the Louisiana Purchase Territories. Brought along by Toussaint Charbonneau, the official expedition guide who purchased her from the Hidatsa Indians, Sacajawea acted as interpreter and guide. Her assistance became vital as she persuaded the Shoshone supply horses and guides to reach the Pacific. Her presence allowed the expedition to pass safely through an area known for inter-tribal warfare.

Connie Douglas Reeves
1997   The Depression ruined Connie's plans to practice law. Instead, in 1936, she joined the staff at Waldemar as head riding instructor and continued in that capacity for over sixty years. She touched the lives of thousands of young women as a role model and a mentor. Connie married in 1942 and with her husband managed a 10,000+ acre ranch for more than forty years. She celebrated her 100th birthday in September 2001.

Gretchen Sammis
1986   A fourth-generation rancher, Gretchen continues the family tradition as owner and operator of the Chase Ranch. Born to be a ranchwoman, she attended college, then taught school while managing the ranch until 1972. A community leader, Gretchen was the first woman to be president of the Northern New Mexico Livestock Association, first woman on the Cimarron School Board and first woman elected to chair the Colfax County Soil and Water Conservation District.

Norma Sanders
1989   Norma was the first professional woman auctioneer. Following in her father's footsteps, she gave up her dream of becoming a concert violinist for the livestock arena. Overcoming existing prejudices against women in the arena, Norma became one of the most popular auctioneers in the country. People attended auctions just to hear the deep voice of *America's Only Cowgirl Auctioneer*, a title she earned during her career in the 1950s and 1960s.

Mari Sandoz   (1896-1966)
1988   Mari published her first story when she was twelve. Growing up on the sandhills of western Nebraska, she wrote of life around her. Mari first gained fame for *Old Jules*, the story of her father and other settlers. She also produced six related books on the relationship of the Indian and white man. Mari won numerous awards for her writing, which presented the drama of man on the Great Plains more accurately and vividly than any writer before her.

Dorothy Satterfield
1993   A popular rodeo performer, Dorothy began her trick riding career at the 1944 Greeley Independence Stampede when she was twelve. Riding Lucky, a horse she raised and trained, Dorothy made rodeos from Texas to California. For more than a decade she worked the rodeo circuit with her husband, Carl. A avid supporter of women's rodeo, Dorothy helped form the GRA before turning her attention to breeding, training and showing quarter horses, winning several AQHA championships.

Dessie Sawyer   (1897-1990)
1981   Dessie was National Democratic Committeewoman and New Mexico's best known political figure for years, but she was first a rancher. She, and her husband, U.D., moved onto their ranch in 1928. With sheer determination and hard work, they paid off the mortgage on the ranch while the country struggled through the Depression. Dessie's work in community activities and public affairs led her into the national political arena because, as Dessie put it, "that's where the fun is."

Fern Sawyer   (1917-1993)
1976   An all-around champion cowgirl, Fern was raised on a ranch where her father insisted she perform as well as the men if she was determined to help with the ranch work. Fern applied this same philosophy to her rodeo career, competing in men's events in rodeos because she found women's events too infrequent and uninspiring. Fern became the first woman to win the National Cutting Horse world title and be inducted into the Cutting Horse Hall of Fame.

Doris Seibold   (1911-1994)
1985   Throughout her teaching career, Doris worked to preserve the culture and folklore of the Indian, Hispanic and Anglo presence in Arizona, instilling a sense of history in her students. Ranch born and raised, she combined her talents to become a successful Quarter Horse breeder and an important historian. Emphasizing the richness of Arizona's history with her publications and teaching, Doris encouraged her students to develop pride in their local community by researching their heritage.

Louise Serpa
1999   Louise was the first woman sanctioned by the RCA to photograph rodeo action inside the arena and spent the next 30 years capturing the action there. Credited with revolutionizing thinking about bodies in motion with her black-and-white images of rodeo events, Louise grew up in New York City, attended Vassar and went west at the first opportunity. This East Coast debutante who became rodeo's premier photographer, started with a $27 camera shooting local cowboys and Junior Rodeos.

Mike Settle
1977   Riding in her first rodeo when she was five, Mike excelled at the sport, winning her first barrel racing championship at 13. During her career, she won titles in Texas, New Mexico, and Oklahoma, including three collegiate titles and making the Ranch Girls' finals four times at Fort Worth. Holding true to her ranching heritage, Mike is still a working cowgirl, continuing to help run the family ranch in the Texas Panhandle.

Reine Hafley Shelton   (1902-1979)
1983   Reine made her vaudeville debut at 3 as part of her mother's sharpshooting act. She broke new ground for women, successfully competing in relay races, trick and bronc riding, and roping events, usually beating the men. Reine taught Tad Lucas trick riding when they both toured with Wild West shows. She rode in the first Madison Square Garden Rodeo. Her trademark stunt had her appearing to fall from her horse's hips, then straightening to a tail stand.

Nancy Sheppard
1991   Nancy headlined at the biggest rodeos at the age of nine, thrilling crowds with her trick riding and roping skills. She rode and roped at most of the major rodeos in the U.S. Her rodeo career began in 1939, lasted until 1961, when she retired to devote more time to ranching and raising her family. Descended from a Texas pioneer ranching family, Nancy was literally raised in a rodeo arena, accompanying her father, a champion calf roper.

Lorraine Shoultz
1981   Known to her audiences as *Baby Lorraine*, she began her riding career at four, performing trick riding on her pony. Lorraine was the star attraction in the Graham Company, a family act featuring eight riding brothers and sisters. Crowned the World Champion Juvenile Trick Rider, Lorraine set national records in trick and fancy riding, roping and bulldogging. Perennial favorites, Lorraine and her siblings became the most popular team of trick riders of the time.

Georgie Sicking
1989   Georgie grew up believing she was born to be a cowhand. But chances to prove herself were scarce for a long time, so Georgie began writing poetry. She eventually achieved her dream of ranching as an equal and her poetry reflects a Western history seen through a ranch hand's eyes. She owned and ran several ranches and her poetry receives national attention with awards like the Gail Garner award for the outstanding working cowboy poet.

Blanche Smith   (1928-1998)
1976   Born into a South Texas ranching family, Blanche was an accomplished cowgirl with a devotion to the sport of rodeo. A champion calf roper, she appeared at all of the major rodeos in Texas, frequently competing against the men. Instrumental in the formation of the Girls Rodeo Association (GRA), Blanche worked as association secretary and then as director to ensure the integrity of the sport and the association.

Elizabeth "Aunt Hank" Boyle Smith   (1848-1925)
1988   Immigrating from Scotland, Aunt Hank followed her brothers to West Texas where she met and married Henry Smith. The first white woman to establish a home on the plains of West Texas, she and her husband also opened the Occidental Hotel, the Texas plain's first hotel. She also taught at the first school. Aunt Hank became doctor and nurse, school teacher, postmistress, hostess and cook to any that crossed her threshold.

Betty Sims Solt
1990   Betty learned the basic skills of good horsemanship while growing up on her family's ranch where she worked alongside her father and five brothers. She began her rodeo career in 1950 at high school rodeo, going on to win numerous awards, including two NIRA Barrel Racing Championships. Betty started teaching in 1964, became a 4-H Club leader and was a charter member of the Berrendo Cowbelles. She also writes cowboy poetry and organized the first New Mexico Cowboy Poetry Roundup.

Agnes Wright Spring   (1894-1988)
1983   Agnes' childhood memories of her parents' stage-line stop, combined with her degrees in English and history led her to author more than twenty books, over 600 feature articles and fiction stories, a play and countless articles in professional journals about the West. The only person to be the official historian of two states, Colorado and Wyoming, she worked in the suffrage movement, trained to be a topographical draftsman and served as Director of the Wyoming Federal Writer's Project.

Rhonda Sedgwick Stearns
1977   Rhonda grew up on a Wyoming ranch learning almost every aspect of ranching and rodeo life starting from the time she could first sit on a horse. Starting young, she won her first horsemanship award at 2 and went on to be a champion barrel racer, a rodeo queen, a rodeo organist, a published western writer and a radio show host. She was the first woman organist to hold a RCA contract card.

Fannie Sperry Steele   (1887-1983)
1978   Fannie took a lifelong fascination of horses and turned it into a rodeo career that included being named World Champion bronc rider and headlining as a sharpshooter. Before she retired from rodeo, Fannie and her husband organized their own Wild West show and a stock company, touring the country. Finally leaving rodeos behind, Fannie went back to Montana to operate a guest ranch, guiding visitors into the Rocky Mountain wilderness until well into her seventies.

Mollie Taylor Stevenson, Sr.
2001   Growing up on the family's 150-year-old ranch, Mollie learned every ranching task from working on windmills to branding cattle. After graduating from Fisk University, Mollie returned to the ranch to preserve her birthright. During the years of segregation, Mollie opened the ranch as a haven for black children who were barred from the city parks. A strong believer in education, she aided many students with the means to have college educations.

Mollie Taylor Stevenson, Jr.
2001   Mollie, Jr., grew up on the family ranch, graduated from TSU, and worked as a professional model before returning to the ranch to preserve her family's legacy. She founded the American Cowboy Museum, which is dedicated to the preservation and understanding of western multicultural heritage and is designed to introduce a new generation to this often overlooked history. Mollie, a sixth-generation rancher, is an active sponsor of FFA and 4-H students.

Hallie Crawford Stillwell   (1897-1983)
1992   Born in 1897, Hallie lived the pioneer life. Adopting the cowboy's pants, shirt and jacket, she ranched beside her husband while maintaining a dignity and femininity that earned her recognition as *Queen of the Big Bend*. Hallie later wrote of her experiences, served as Justice of the Peace, and opened a museum to preserve her life's treasures.

Anne Stradling   (1913-1992)
1987   Creator of the Museum of the Horse, the first U.S. museum dedicated to the horse, Anne began her collection of horse-related items as a young girl in New Jersey. The daughter of a prominent land developer, she participated in her first horse show at six, later learning to trick ride with the 101 Ranch Show, and competed in calf roping. Her horse museum began as a one-room exhibit but grew into a collection valued in the millions of dollars. It is now located in Ruidoso, New Mexico.

Mabel Strickland   (1897-1976)
1992   Mable bested most cowboys in rodeo events, including bronc and steer riding, roping and trick and roman riding. She began her career riding relay races, but soon added steer roping and trick riding, winning championships in all three events and earning considerable fame. Noticed by the booming movie industry, Mable found Hollywood success and founded the Association of Film Equestriennes. Mable retired in 1941 to raise Appaloosa horses.

Carrie Ingalls Swanzey   (1870-1946)
1984   Born during her parents' stay in Kansas, Carrie, third daughter of the Ingalls, grew up in DeSmet, South Dakota. Upon graduating from high school, she went to work for the local newspaper, which led to her management of several newspapers. Moving to Keystone, Colorado, to run a paper, she met and married a miner, David Swanzey. At Keystone, she became an active leader in the community and her church.

Wilma Standard Tate
1985   Known as the *Texas Tomboy* during her rodeo career, Wilma taught herself to rope using a rented donkey for practice. She became a champion roper and trick rider, dazzling audiences with her Roman riding act and her skill with a horse. She also trained and showed cutting horses before establishing her own riding school in California, sharing her knowledge of the show ring with her students. She has won worldwide acclaim for her skill as a teacher.

Jerry Portwood Taylor
1986   Learning to ride early, Jerry's skill on a horse carried her far from her hometown of Seymour, Texas. Her trick riding and roping landed her jobs as a Pangburn Candy Girl, work with Tex Ritter in England and performing with Gene Autry's rodeo. Known for her flamboyant style of riding and dressing, Jerry traveled the county in her trademark convertible Cadillac with matching horse trailer. Jerry remains a working cowgirl, running her own ranching operation.

Ruth Thompson   (1908-1990)
1990   Ruth and her husband, Cal, were instrumental in the development and registry of the American Albino horse. The breed, also known as the American White, had its origin on the Thompson's White Horse Ranch in Nebraska. A farmer's daughter, Ruth grew up working horses in the field, but it wasn't until her marriage that she became interested in breeding horses. She also established a training and riding center on the ranch to teach underprivileged children horsemanship.

Sissy Thurman   (1934-1968)
1975   Sissy began riding horses at five years old and competed in her first barrel race event at eleven. Born in Galveston, she served as rodeo queen for local rodeo and stock shows, and was a tap dancer and teacher before she began to rodeo professionally. Sissy went on to become one of the country's top barrel racers, at one point setting the fastest time in NFR barrel racing to that date. She also held barrel racing clinics and served as barrel racing director for the GRA.

Marie Cordner Tyler   (1908-2002)
1988   Known as the *first lady of beef promotion*, Marie knew about cattle and horses from her youth on the family ranch. She brought the first Santa Gertrudis cattle to North Dakota and joined with other ranchers to promote beef sales and distribution. Active in pleasure-riding events, Marie and her husband Jim were also among the first to raise registered Quarter Horses in North Dakota. Marie served as the first female chair of the National Livestock and Meat Board.

Barbara Van Cleve
1995   Barbara's photographs of the ranching west are authentic images accurately portraying ranch life in the modern West. Raised on the family's Montana ranch, she learned ranch life as a participant, with photography as an avocation. Barbara taught English Literature and Photography at DePaul University in Chicago, becoming the youngest Dean of Women in the U.S. She retired from teaching to pursue photography full-time and has gained international acclaim.

Alice Van-Springsteen
1998   From Alice's debut as a trick rider in 1930 through her later competitions in trick, fancy and relay riding, she performed in major rodeos from New York to Australia. A world champion trick rider, Alice was only the second woman to receive a trainer's license. She eventually began working in the movie industry, becoming one of the most sought after stunt riders in Hollywood. Alice, with Ronald Reagan, helped organize the Screen Actors Guild.

Hope Kemnitz Varner
1988   Born in Milwaukee, Hope always felt the lure of the West. With her husband, Tex, she spent her life promoting Western life. A talented musician and singer, Hope hosted a radio show and directed a working guest ranch. She related stories and songs of the West to thousands of children and adults, also teaching horsemanship to many. Hope and her family produced rodeos (co-produced 1955 GRA rodeo) and Wild West shows at their own arena.

Karen Womack Vold
1978   The daughter of a rodeo clown, Karen taught herself to trick ride and, when she was eleven, began a twelve year career. She was instrumental in forming *The Flying Cimarrons*, a group that brought trick riding back into prominence for several years. The formation of this group was an innovation for rodeo shows because it hired out as a complete act instead of several individual acts. Karen retired from performing upon marriage, but continues to be involved in rodeo business through producing rodeos and trick riding clinics.

Dora Waldrop
1979   From the time she went to work on horseback when she was three bringing in milkcows to competing in barrel racing at 76, Dora was a standout Texas horsewoman who consistently won on the horses she trained. A fierce promoter for barrel racing, she was the first to convince Texas Panhandle rodeos to include girls barrel racing as an event. While recovering from a riding injury, Dora turned to writing horsemanship articles for the major horse publications.

Cindy Walker
1998   Called the greatest female country composer in history, Cindy wrote her first song when she was twelve. She is the only songwriter to have Top Ten hits in five successive decades. Cindy has written more than 500 classic songs and was inducted into the Country Music Hall of Fame. A recording artist in her own right, Cindy wrote songs for Bob Wills, appeared in Gene Autry movies and hosted her own radio show in California.

Ruth Parton Webster   (1895-1978)
1988   Called the *Mother of Thoroughbred Racing*, Ruth began racing Thoroughbreds on the Yakima Reservation in Washington when she was thirteen. Her successes on the track led to rodeo appearances, and to the sport of relay racing. With six fast Canadian fillies, Ruth brought her winning abilities to the pony-express style races, soon earning the title World's Champion Woman Relay Racer. She trained and raced Thoroughbreds in Canada and Mexico before retiring in 1929.

Joan Wells
1989   To watch Joan, the 1979 Women's World Champion Trick Roper, perform is to witness an authentic link to the early Wild West shows. Her interest in roping began in childhood, when, with coaching from a cousin, Joan began performing at fairs, rodeos and on television. Devoted to the art, she teaches clinics and writes articles on roping to help preserve a vanishing piece of the West.

Ernestine Chesser Williams
1983   Ernestine taught school for thirty-three years before retiring and starting a writing career. After a full life of rural schools, farming and raising livestock in New Mexico, where her parents were early pioneers, she set out to record and preserve the histories of local people and events. Ernestine published five books and numerous articles about New Mexico's heritage, becoming known for her accurate recounting of Southwest ranching culture.

Mary Nan West   (1925-2001)
1998   Raised by her grandparents as heir to the Rafter S Ranch, Mary grew up shunning society socials and events for ranch work. The hard work and values learned on the ranch made her into one of the most influential women in Texas. Among other firsts, she was the first female president of the San Antonio Livestock Exposition, the first woman to serve on the Texas Animal Health Commission and the first woman chairman of the Texas A&M Board of Regents.

Nancy Bragg Witmer
1997   Nancy began her trick riding career on a borrowed horse at the Texas Cowboy Reunion in Stamford, Texas. Trained in tap and acrobatic dancing and educated in drama at Brenau College, Nancy worked rodeos as a child trick roper. She discovered trick riding, invented a signature stunt, the *Falling Tower* and became the feature attraction in the major rodeos by 17. An accomplished horsewoman, Nancy also won the GRA World Champion Cutting Horse title twice.

Vivian White   (1912-1999)
1985   Vivian was the winner of the last cowgirl bronc riding event at Madison Square Garden in 1941. Her rodeo career began when she was 15, riding steers and buffaloes in exhibition rides. A champion trick rider and bronc rider who held the distinction of never being bucked off in the arena, her rodeo career lasted eighteen years. She retired with the birth of her daughter, focusing on raising cattle and quarter horses.

Jackie Worthington   (1925-1987)
1975   Jackie was instrumental in the formation of the GRA, helping to plan and form the association and serving two terms as president. Holding 23 world championships from a thirteen year rodeo career, Jackie learned to ride on her parent's ranch, using everything from the milk-pen cows to the broodmares to train. A graduate of Texas State College for Women and an accomplished musician, Jackie eventually retired from rodeo to take over management of the family ranch.

Narcissa Prentiss Whitman   (1808-1847)
1979   As the new wife of a missionary to the Cayuse Indians in Oregon, Narcissa was one of first two white women to cross the Rocky Mountains. Her journals and letters provide historic insight into life in the frontier. The New York-born daughter of a judge, Narcissa settled into a cabin in the Walla Walla area, where, after her own daughter died, she raised eleven adopted children until her death in an 1847 massacre.

Sydna Yokley Woodyard   (1932-1959)
1977   Sydna was one of the founders of the American Quarter Horse Association and a noted quarter horse breeder, but it was her rodeo career that brought her fame. Raised on a Texas ranch, she was a top-notch calf roper and trick rider in the 1940s and 1950s whose performances at Madison Square Garden and Boston caught the attention of Hollywood and the most popular national magazines, helping to popularize women's roping contests.

Laura Ingalls Wilder   (1867-1957)
1984   Best known for her *Little House on the Prairie* books, Laura was born in a log cabin in Wisconsin and saw the frontier as her family traveled west as pioneer settlers. It is on these experiences that Laura based her books. She captured the successive phases of the American frontier by preserving her own memories of her travels. Though her first book was not published until she was 68, Laura continued to write until after she was 76.

Nellie Snyder Yost   (1905-1992)
1992   Nellie published her first book when she was 46, a collection of the stories told by her father about early ranching life. She went on to write eleven more books and numerous articles about the people and history of the West. Raised in northwest Nebraska and home schooled until she was ten, Nellie was honored with many prestigious awards for her ability to capture the essence of the wild west. She is celebrated as Nebraska's pioneer storyteller.

Eleanor McClintock Williams   (1906-1979)
1986   Eleanor's life epitomized the strong, independent western woman. The daughter of wealthy Pittsburgh artists, Eleanor became enthused with life in the West as a teenager. She became a champion trick rider, performing on the rodeo circuit, Wild West shows and circuses. She purchased and built a ranch during the Depression, raised five children, ran for the New Mexico Senate, was a published writer and became a recognized artist.

Isora DeRacy Young
1979   Isora's love for ranching, horses, and roping made her a pioneer. Isora is a champion calf roper and barrel racer from a time when women in rodeo were very rare. She began competing in the early 1930s and was promoted as one of only two cowgirl calf ropers in the world. She followed the rodeo circuit all across the country and aided in the organization of the GRA, until she retired to ranching.

Florence Youree
1996   Early in her career, Florence competed in barrel races with no set pattern and sometimes ran around old water heaters. She dedicated herself to promoting the sport and bringing it from a seldom featured novelty event to standardized competition. Florence also led the GRA from a fledgling organization to one of national prominence. With her husband, she organized the Barrel Futurities of America, the Oklahoma Youth Rodeo Association, and the Youree Horsemanship Camps.

Jan Youren
1993   Jan excels in every rodeo event, especially bareback bronc and bull riding. She has competed for over four decades, winning top honors and world titles in the WPRA. A fervent advocate of the sport since her first bareback bronc ride, Jan also holds clinics to teach young women the art of riding rough stock. Centering her life between rodeo and family, Jan's dedication and goodwill personify to many what it means to be a cowgirl.

Messages from our supporters

CONGRATULATIONS COWGIRLS!

WE TIP OUR HATS TO THE OPENING OF THE NATIONAL COWGIRL MUSEUM AND HALL OF FAME.

The can-do spirit that built the American West is alive and well at JPMorgan Chase. You'll find it in our people, including Elaine Agather, Chairman & CEO of JPMorgan Chase – Dallas and Managing Director of the JPMorgan Private Bank– Southwest. A board member of the National Cowgirl Museum and Hall of Fame and a fan of cowgirls everywhere, Elaine brings a passion and commitment to her work you won't find in a typical banker.

Ready for real financial success? Saddle up with JPMorgan Chase.

JPMorganChase

We salute the great women of the American West.

Star-Telegram
What do you want to know?

GENUINE SPIRIT

The American Quarter Horse has it. You have it.
Partner up with America's Horse and show your spirit.

AMERICAN QUARTER HORSE ASSOCIATION

Discover the spirit of the American Quarter Horse.
Call AQHA at 1-800-414-RIDE or visit us at www.aqha.com

Let Freedom Ride

DOUBLE·D RANCH

*Double D Ranch
Apparel and Home
Collection*

800.899.3379

www.ddranchwear.com

Powerfully built.

Gentle by nature.

Spectacular by design.

Whether your passion is cutting, driving, or simply enjoying the back of a good horse, there is no better companion than today's American Paint Horse.

Bred to do it all
—beautifully

American Paint Horse Association
40th Anniversary
Celebrating a Heritage of Color

P.O. Box 961023 ◆ Fort Worth, Texas 76161-0023
(817) 834-2742 ◆ www.apha.com

CONGRATULATIONS
NATIONAL COWGIRL MUSEUM AND HALL OF FAME

We are proud to have played a part in honoring women of the American West.

West Office Exhibition Design
www.woed.com

Hawn Holt
Cross Triangle Ranch

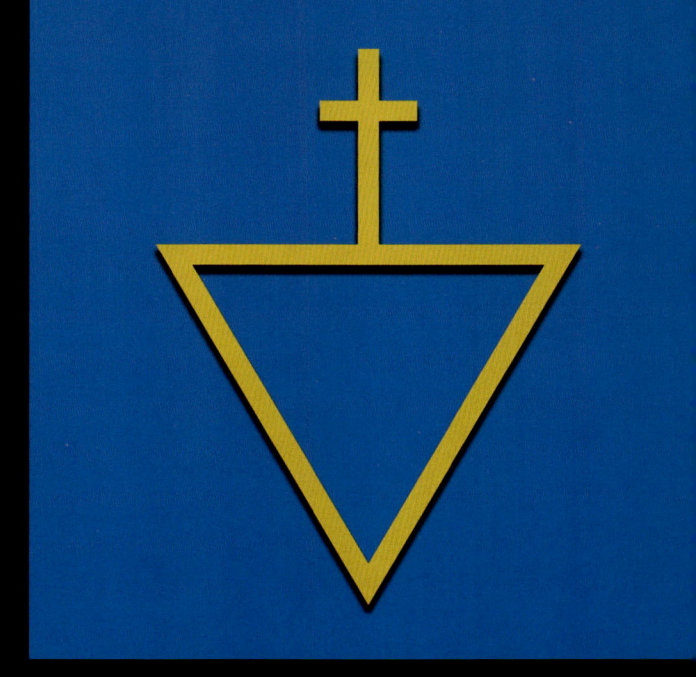

Congratulations!

LINK LAW FIRM

KML

Alice and Ken Link

GideonToal

500 West Seventh Street
Suite 1400
Fort Worth Texas 76102
817.335.4991
www.gideontoal.com

Architecture • Engineering • Planning
Interiors • Landscape Architecture

Feasibility Analysis ▪ Planning and Construction Consultation ▪ Process Facilitation

Ooohh, Give Me a Home.

Linbeck couldn't be prouder to be the Construction Manager for the new home of the National Cowgirl Museum and Hall of Fame. Of course, as planners and builders of such masterpieces as the Bass Performance Hall, the newly renovated Amon Carter Museum and the new Modern Art Museum of Fort Worth, we know a thing or two about building cultural monuments. Let us help make your vision a reality with our collaborative TeamBuild® approach. Like the courageous women in the National Cowgirl Hall of Fame, we're true pioneers.

Linbeck
Uncommon Collaboration

FORT WORTH   HOUSTON   BOSTON   WWW.LINBECK.COM

Project Management ▪ Construction Management ▪ Development ▪ Commissioning

The Professional Rodeo Cowboys Association

Maintaining pro rodeo's history. Ensuring its future.

prca PRORODEO

101 Pro Rodeo Drive
Colorado Springs, Colo. 80919
(719) 593-8840
www.prorodeo.com

Ranch house Trading Co.

Home Collections

200 W. Exchange Ave.
Fort Worth, Texas 76106
817-625-2341
In The Historic Stockyards

Opening July 2002

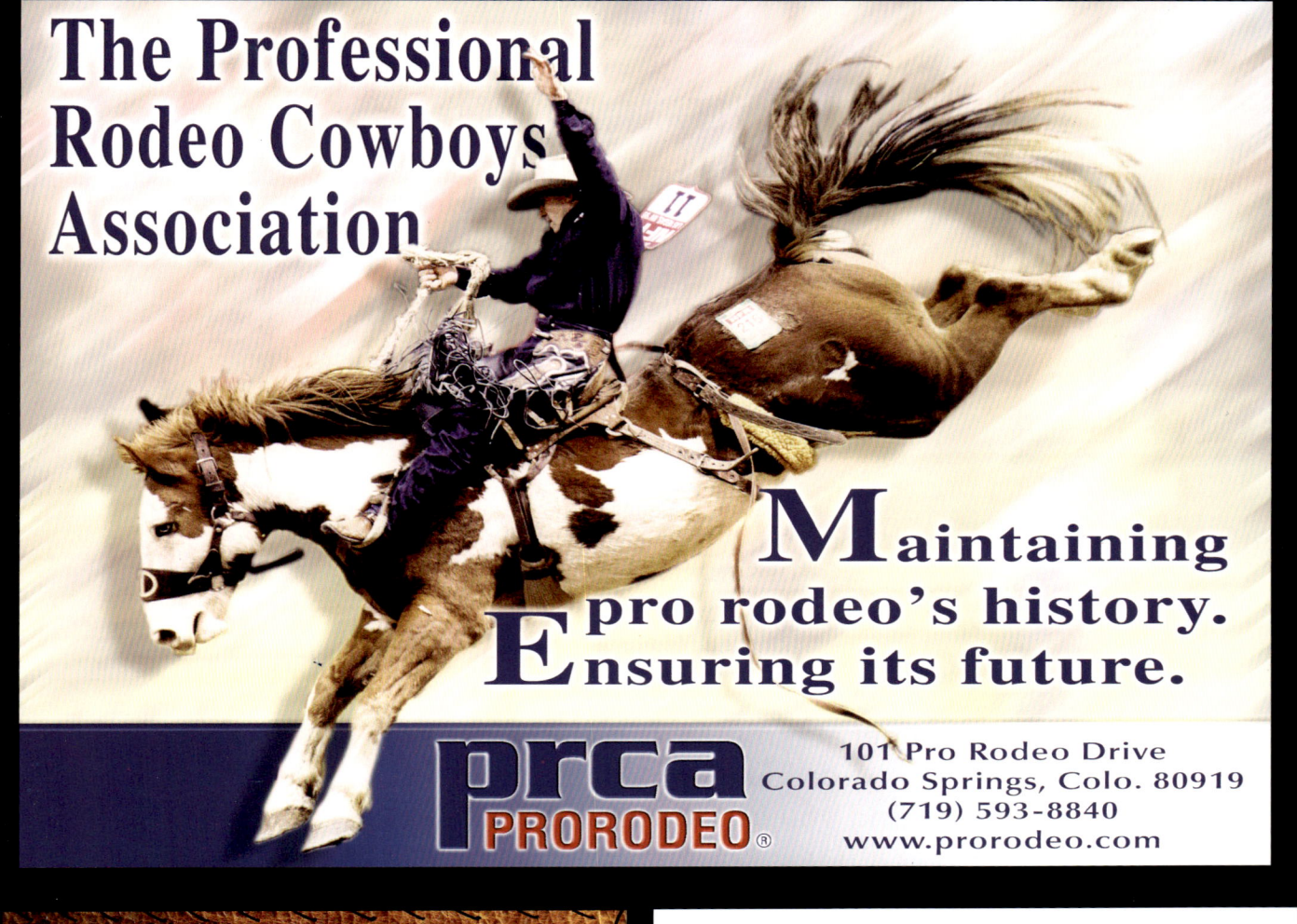

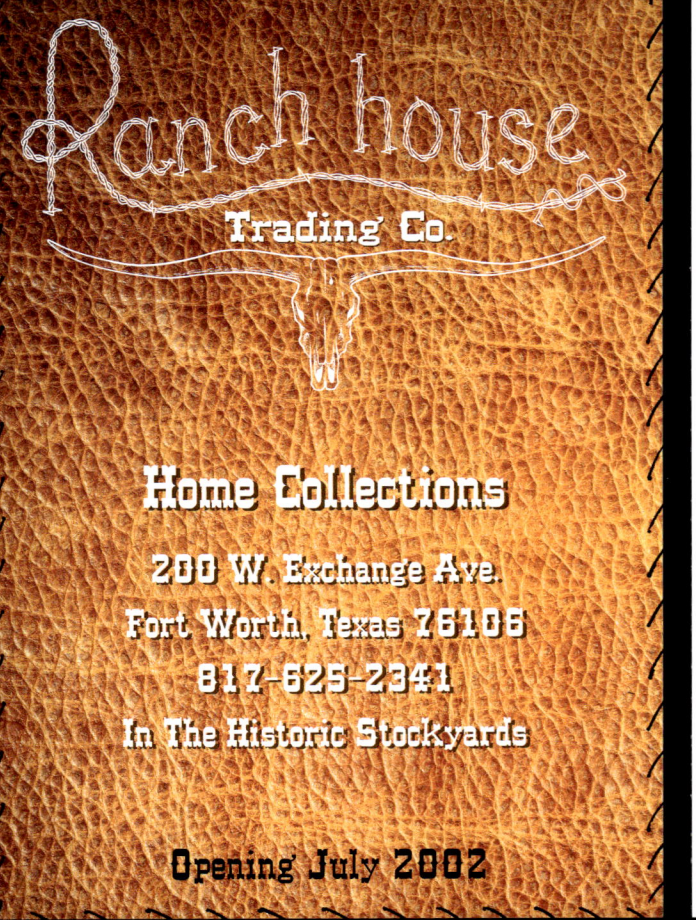

SUMMIT CONSULTANTS, INC.

Celebrating the Spirit and History of the American Cowgirl.

Summit Consultants – providing mechanical, electrical and plumbing engineering design to the National Cowgirl Museum and Hall of Fame.

BE YOURSELF
Georgie Sicking

When I was young and foolish
the women said to me,
"Take off those spurs and comb
your hair, if a lady you will be.

"Forget about those cowboy ways.
Come and sit awhile.
We will try to clue you in on women's
ways and wiles.

"Take off that Levi's jumper, put up
those batwing chaps.
Put on a little makeup and we can get a
date for you perhaps.

"Forget about that roping, that will make
callouses on your hands.
And you know it takes soft fingers
if you want to catch a man.

"Do away with that Stetson hat for
it will crush your curls.
And even a homely cowboy wouldn't
date a straight-haired girl."

Now, being young and foolish,
I went my merry way,
And I guess I never wore a dress
until my wedding day.

Now I tell my children,
"No matter what you do,
stand up straight and tall.
Be you and only you.

For if the Lord had meant us all
to be alike and the same rules to keep,
He would have bonded us all together
just like a flock of sheep."

COLOPHON

Two thousand five hundred copies of this catalogue were printed at Authentic Press, Arlington, Texas in May of 2002. The paper used was LOE 80# text, printed on a waterless press. The book was designed by Michael T. Ricker with the assistance of
Karen Mullarkey.